The Quiet Rebel

THE QUIET REBEL

How to Survive as a Woman & Businessperson

GLYNIS M. BREAKWELL

Grove Press, Inc., New York

First Grove Press Edition 1986
First Printing 1986
ISBN: 0-394-55560-0
Library of Congress Catalog Card Number: 86-45431

Library of Congress Cataloging-in-Publication Data

Breakwell, Glynis M. (Glynis Marie)
    The quiet rebel.

    1. Women—Employment.   2. Sex role in the work
environment.   I. Title.
HD6053.B736   1986   331.4'01'9   86-45431
ISBN 0-394-55560-0
ISBN 0-394-62282-0 (pbk.)

Printed in the United States of America

Grove Press, Inc., 920 Broadway
New York, N.Y. 10010

5   4   3   2   1

To my mother, Vera Breakwell, who taught me early that you are as good as you bloody well think you are; a lesson every Quiet Rebel has to learn.

Contents

6. NO-GO EMOTIONS   128
      Why are No-Go Emotions so Dangerous?   128
      Why are Women so Subject to the No-Go Emotions? 131
      Breaking Tradition and the No-Go Emotions   134
      Controlling the No-Go Emotions   141
      Power Talk   143

7. SELF-EXERCISES   149
      Self-Maintenance   150
      Negativism   153
      Stress   157
      Personality and Stress   159
      Habitual Coping Strategies   160
      Focus for Coping   162
      Stress Management   163
            Systematic Desensitisation   164
            Stress Inoculation   166
            Biofeedback   167
            Cognitive Approaches   170
            Social Skills Training   173
      Blocking Stress Management   179
      Self-Esteem and Impression Management   180
      Exercising the Self   184

8. CHANGING OTHERS   186
      Becoming Persuasive   186
      It's not what you say, it's the way that you say it   188
      Frightening them into Submission   190
      Prime Targets for Persuasion   191
      Attitudes and Actions   192
      Unanticipated Side-Effects   194

9. THE QUIET REBEL   196
      Crises for the Quiet Rebel   198
      Halos and Horns   200

Preface

This is a book about women who do jobs normally done only by men. Sometimes it is the type of job they do which sets them apart: they go to sea in the merchant marine; they pilot passenger planes; they drive underground trains; they operate the giant machines in the print industry; they direct cinema films; or they lead tourist safaris in far-away places. These women are unusual because they do jobs which are tradition-ally and stereotypically male. At other times, more often, it is the status they attain which sets some women apart. Even where women are well-represented in an industry or service, they tend to congregate in the low-status jobs. They are nurses, teachers, secretaries and clerks rather than hospital administ-rators, heads of schools, managing directors, or partners in a law firm. Women who do gain positions of power and authority are still in a minority. Women who are unusual either because of the type of job they do or because they have gained status in male-dominated jobs are the focus of this book.

Such women are breaking long-established traditions in the workplace and often in their own homes. They are challenging the image that society has of the appropriate place and occupation for a woman. They are rebels. Yet, in essence, the majority are *quiet rebels*. They are not militant campaigners for a change in the position of women as a whole in our society. They do not band together to induce governments to alter legislation. They initiate no social movements, create no inflammatory propaganda, and disturb no peace. Their rebellion is a personal affair, not warfare waged on behalf of others. They pursue their own career interests with the minimal necessary antagonism of the sensibilities of society. They are individualists seeking individualised solutions to the problems they encounter. Basically, they are just ordinary women doing jobs extra-ordinary for women. They certainly have no overwhelming political motive for their choice of job. They would mostly consider themselves egalitarian liberals, and not radical, aggressive or anti-anything. While denying any ulterior political objective, the quiet rebel is aware of the wider implications of her personal stance. She knows deep down that she is in the vanguard of social change. She understands that her rebellion, if successful, will make it much easier for others to follow in her footsteps later. She has some inkling of her role as a model for other younger women. But these effects of her actions are incidental. Her main concern is with her own personal development and success in a job that she chooses to do. Achieving this is difficult enough without worrying about changing the world at the same time.

This book is about the barriers which the quiet rebel has to overcome. These barriers are both social and psychological. She has to withstand the prejudices of others, institutionalised in the structure of sex-role stereotypes, the family, the edu-cation system, and vocational guidance. Possibly more horrendous is the task she has in overcoming the psychological obstacles that she herself has constructed over the years: her fear of success; her tendency towards self-handicapping; and her learned helplessness. In describing these barriers fully in the first three chapters, my purpose is to alert both the actual and the potential quiet rebel to the obstacles which face her. Understanding the roots of these obstacles is the first step along the route to overcoming them.

The rest of the book is devoted to exploring the dynamics underlying relationships which develop at work, including sexual harassment, and to describing how work roles can be altered and ritualised patterns of interaction remodelled. Strategies are described for dealing with the self-doubt, self-blame and guilt many quiet rebels experience. This is a precursor to the discussion of how the quiet rebel needs to evolve a strong self-concept invested with self-esteem, and how impression management and strategies for coping with stress might be used. Although most of the suggestions for action on the part of the quiet rebel revolve around how she might change herself and her own behaviour, the penultimate chapter concentrates upon the techniques of persuasion which she might use in changing the attitudes and actions of other people.

From this brief summary, it can be seen that the book has dual objectives: to describe the position of the quiet rebel, and to suggest how she might exert greater control over her own fate. Clearly as long as she remains a quiet rebel, the courses of action open to her are limited; the range of her successes is largely personal. The quiet rebel who effectively utilises the coping strategies and the persuasive techniques suggested may become dissatisfied with that range of success. Through understanding the nature of her own problems further, she may come to appreciate that the barriers are not individualised, they are shared by all women, and she may come to feel that recourse to individual solutions is not enough. Such realisation could metamorphose the quiet rebel and give birth to an unquiet rebel who will need a whole new set of weapons not described in this book.

Chapter One

BREAKING TRADITION

Who is the Quiet Rebel?

Every woman is a rebel. Every woman knows that just because she is a woman, there are constraints upon how she ought to think, feel and act. Every woman, at some time in her life, resists these constraints. Women differ only in the target of their rebellion, its visibility and its longevity.

Not every woman is a quiet rebel. Quiet rebels are unlikely to identify themselves as rebels at all. Few would self-consciously regard themselves as trail-blazing Che Guevaras undermining the fabric of society. They break with tradition for practical, everyday reasons in pursuit of their personal goals, not through some great ideological passion or with grand political motive. Their prime purpose is certainly not to bring about change for all women. Yet, like the small pebble which unleashes the landslide, their individual acts of self-interest can initiate a chain of events which ultimately affects all women. They resist the pressures to conform and thus bring about change for themselves and others without necessarily explaining them-selves or uniting with others: hence the legitimacy of the title 'quiet rebels'.

There are as many sites for resistance as there are facets to society's image of a woman's role. This role description encompasses everything from the minutiae of psychological functioning (level of emotionality, assertiveness, and intellectual abilities) to physical form (appropriate shape, size and adornment), and from close interpersonal relationships (direction of sexuality, familial obligations, and friendship patterns) to level of economic and political activity. The precise parameters of the role description differ across cultures, generations and socio-economic classes, which means that the form of female rebellion will also vary with culture, generation and class.

Make no mistake about it, the role is meant to be performed. Sex roles are no theoretical fiction concocted by psychologists or sociologists or even by militant feminists. They have just baptised a creature that women have always been able to delineate. When asked, women can describe the dimensions of their own sex role. What is more, they can describe the punishments incurred for any infringements: the emotional blackmail and social shame. There is some latitude of freedom for eccentricities in performance, but these are severely limited in most settings.

It is fashionable to suggest that sex roles are becoming less potent determiners of behaviour and that the dichotomy of male and female images is crumbling. Out of their ashes, it is proposed, will arise the androgynous person who embodies the most positive psychological characteristics of both masculine and feminine types. The evidence for the declining impact of sex-role prescriptions is rather slender. The characteristics comprising the sex roles may be changing: women are expected to be more aggressive, men more emotional than before. This does not necessarily imply sameness or the eradication of distinctions in sex roles. For instance, the interpretation of the meaning of aggression from a woman may be quite different from that of a man. More importantly, the argument that the characteristics prescribed are changing is quite separate from that about their importance in controlling an individual's self-concept and behaviour. There is no evidence that the new prescriptions are less powerful than the old. Indeed, the contradictions between the old and the new are a source of considerable distress for some people, who have lost the singular guideline for action which previously applied.

One of the most prominent components of sex-role prescriptions has concerned work. A clear division of labour by sex has operated in the home and outside it. Women's work and men's work have overlapped at the edges, but occupational segregation has dominated. Yet one of the most frequent and visible arenas for the operation of the quiet rebel is found in this element of the sex role. Women do men's work. The purpose of much of this book is to describe the barriers which have to be overcome by the quiet rebel in her attempt to get men's work, the problems likely once she has it, and some survival strategies that she could use.

Women's Work, Men's Work

There are three sorts of occupational segregation according to sex: horizontal segregation, vertical segregation, and social segregation. Horizontal segregation refers to differences in the type of work done. Women congregate in non-manual occupations, men in those involving manual work. In 1982, US Department of Labor figures showed that 34.7 per cent of employed women were clerical workers; 6.8 per cent worked in sales; and 17.1 per cent worked in service industries like education, health and welfare. Less than one-third of men have non-manual occupations.

Yet horizontal segregation is rarely complete. By 1971, only 2 per cent of occupations were wholly male in the US, while 12 per cent had as many as 70 per cent women workers (this is based on 223 occupations identified at census, Hakim 1979). Twenty-six per cent of all occupations had more women workers than men. These include jobs which are almost exclusively female preserves. For example, by 1981, the US Department of Labor reported that 93 per cent of all bank tellers were women. Although there are a vast number of occupations in which men predominate, there are relatively few in which there are no women at all.

Vertical segregation is more virulent. This concerns status differentials within a single type of work. Basically women do the jobs of lower status, and men predominate in the higher grades within each occupational group. There is an unambiguous trend over recent years towards greater vertical segregation in manual, managerial, administrative, and lower professional and technical occupations. In 1981, only 7 in 100 women in the US held management positions and this figure has risen less than 3 points in the last 20 years.

The status differential is paralleled by differential earning power. In the US, at a rough approximation across a range of industries, women have earned only two-thirds as much as men, and this has been the case for as long as records have been kept. Until recently, this figure has been compounded for minority women who have earned on average just over two-thirds the wage of white women. Even if experience, qualifications, type of work and length of employment are held constant, the average man will earn 10 per cent more than a comparable woman (based on recent US and British surveys).

Social segregation occurs when both sexes do a particular job and when both can gain positions of power doing it, but where things are so arranged that they never work together. The women work separately from the men; direct comparisons between them are consequently impossible. This often happens in those 12 per cent of occupations where women form more than 70 per cent of the labor force; for instance, in the case of registered nurses, elementary school teachers, waitresses, hairdressers, and workers in the rag trade.

Horizontal, vertical and social segregation pinpoint the nature of women's work and men's work. The vital question is what happens when a woman breaks the rules: entering a sexually-atypical job, gaining promotion and power within an occupation where women occupy the basement, choosing to pursue her work where men of equivalent status and skills do theirs.

Rebellion at Work means Rebellion at Home and in the Community

One's working life is not cordonned off from the rest by some impregnable barrier. What happens at work has knock-on effects in the family and in the community. The acceptable and traditional patterns of women's work are shadowed by familial and community arrangements which they accommodate. So, for instance, married women with children of school age have normally been expected to take part-time jobs that could be bent around the family's timetable. Women have regarded the job of their spouse as more important than their own (not surprisingly, since he has been likely to earn much more and have better chances of promotion). This has resulted in women being willing to sacrifice their own job if required in order to service his. Consequently, women have been considered less reliable long-term bets by employers. Equally, they have been regarded as unwilling to take on added responsibilities or greater work commitments because they give priority to their domestic obligations. Ironically, the woman without familial responsibilities, the single childless woman, is still suspect: marriage and pregnancy are considered ultimate inevitabilities, providing the rationale for withholding promotion and opportunity.

The woman who breaks the rules of women's work throws these domestic preconceptions to the wind. She may not intend to, but the fact is that she does. She is bound to rearrange relationships in her home and will often surprise, even offend, neighbours, relatives, and community worthies. Simple things like visiting friends, buying new shoes for the children, supporting community charities, maintaining the garden, trips to the hairdresser change when a woman does a man's work. The sheer number of hours free in the day dramatically drops. So purely practical changes occur. Some of these changes would occur simply because the woman was working, regardless of the type of work and irrespective of whether she was doing a job normally done by a man. However, the practical implications of supplanting a man at work tend to be greater, because often it entails longer working hours and deeper levels of responsibility and power. There is less time and less energy left for domestic and community commitments. This is true whether the woman is married or single. Remaining unmarried or childless is no safeguard against the pressures which exist to comply with traditional female roles. After a woman reaches a 'certain age', these pressures are multiplied if she remains single or has no children. For her there are the dual pressures to conform at work and to conform in the home.

The psychological changes consequent upon failing to conform are much more vital than the practical ones. A woman who breaks with tradition starts to think about herself in new ways. She might recognise herself as competent, autonomous and even successful in her own right for the first time. These new insights can permeate all aspects of her life. They may come as a shock to the people she has lived with who rather like the old self. They will certainly alter relationships she holds dear. The changes may evolve naturally or they may require a lot of effort. In the latter case, the quiet rebel at work has to become a rebel, quiet or otherwise, at home.

The Changing Life Cycle of a Woman at Work

The typical working life of a woman is characterised by two phases: pre-childrearing and post-childrearing. A survey conducted in Britain in 1984 showed that 93 per cent of childless women were in work or actively seeking a job. Marriage itself is not the prime reason a woman leaves work nowadays, having a child is. In fact, in 1979, 51.3 per cent of married women were in paid employment. There have been stark changes in this respect over the last sixty years: in 1951 the comparable figure was 21.7 per cent and in 1911 only 9.6 per cent. By 1991, the Department of Employment predicts that married women will comprise nearly 30 per cent of the country's labour force.

Due to the arrival of children, most women drop out of the workforce in their mid- to late-twenties. The length of time they remain out depends on the ages and number of their children. About one-third of women with a child under four years will be at work, by the time the youngest child is ten as many as 70 per cent will be working, and 80 per cent are back by the child's fifteenth birthday.

The speed with which women return to work after child-rearing is increasing. Today's mothers get a job several years before their own mothers would have done so. Comparisons across generations show that women in their thirties and forties are much more likely now to be back in work. But they most frequently return to part-time work; half of the married women who work are part-timers, and most of these have two or more young children.

The Effects of Equal Opportunities Legislation

Several laws seek to ensure equal employment opportunities. Title VII of the Civil Rights Act of 1964 prohibits discrimination in employment based on sex, race, color, religion or national origin. It encompasses wages, promotion, the provision of training, and conditions of service (including social conditions such that cases against sexual harassment may be pursued under this act). The Equal Pay Act of 1963 further prohibited unequal pay and benefits for men and women working in the same place and whose jobs entail similar skill, effort and responsibility. The jobs need not be identical but differences should be of no practical importance for the act to operate.

Two other pieces of legislation have supported women's call for equality in employment opportunity. The Pregnancy Discrimination Act of 1978 ensures pregnant women have the same legal rights as other employees with regard to hiring or firing, promotion or pay, and with respect to benefits or leave (pregnancy is treated as equivalent to any temporary disability). Executive Order 11246 requires companies that have business contracts with the federal government to take positive action to correct the effects of past discriminatory employment practices. Typically, they are required to produce Affirmative Action Plans and make these available to employees. The Plan identifies where women or minority group members are not sufficiently represented and details timetables for eliminating imbalances.

There are a number of institutions responsible for the enforcement of this legislation. At the Federal level, the Civil Service Commission, the Equal Employment Opportunities Commission, the Department of Justice and the Department of Labor are all involved. The Civil Rights Commission and Women's Bureau of the Department of Labor carry out research and offer policy advice to politicians. In addition, each government department has its own equal opportunities office. Most states and some cities have their own offices of fair employment, equal opportunities and contract compliance.

During the first ten years of enforcement, the lack of coordination between a multiplicity of agencies hindered effective action. In 1978, the system was rationalised by President Carter with the Equal Employment Opportunity Commission (EEOC) taking a prime role.

Calculating the effects of the legislation is not easy. Surveys of these effects (see Meehan, 1985, for instance) suggest that most *overt* forms of discrimination in employment have disappeared, and some job opportunities that had previously been closed are now open to women. By the mid-1970s women had increased their share of some occupations in which men predominate; for example, in the professional, craft and operator categories. Between 1960 and 1970, the rates of increase of women in accountancy, architecture, engineering, physics, the law and judiciary quadrupled. There were comparable sharp rises in female enrollments on degree courses leading to such careers; a move facilitated by the flexibility of course structures in the US universities and colleges. In the manual sector, similar rates of change occurred during the same decade in the skilled trades, especially among electricians, car mechanics, painters, toolmakers, plumbers, carpenters, machinists, compositors and typesetters. Overall the rate of increase in skilled female labour was 8 times that of skilled male labour. Despite all this, it is important to recognise that while rates rose rapidly, the absolute numbers of women concerned are very small. Moreover, since 1975, with the onset of recession, the improvements in the manual sector have lowered dramatically though the situation in the managerial, executive and administrative areas remains more optimistic.

Success regarding pay has been limited by the fact that large numbers of women are not, in practice, covered by the legislation because they work in 'segregated jobs', where no comparable males work. Job segregation has clearly continued despite the acts, and women in the early 1980s still congregate in the low-paid industries in lower-grade jobs.

In fact, the difference between men's and women's pay, in all major occupational groups except service workers, has remained virtually the same since 1963. In 1963, female sales workers earned an average annual income of 39 per cent less than male sales workers and professional women earned 64.8 per cent less than their male counterparts. In 1973, the same groups were still earning 37.8 per cent and 63.8 per cent less, respectively. From 1973 to 1983, the aggregate difference hovered around 60 per cent. Despite the persistent differences in pay for men and women, the differences in incomes of white and minority group women narrowed from 25 per cent in 1967 to less than 7 per cent in 1974.

There have been numerous attempts to explain the disappointing effects of the Equal Pay Act. Some suggest that, as the Equal Opportunities legislation attracts more women into the labour market to look for work in new realms of activity, they will be working in junior positions for lower salaries while establishing a foothold in the job and this, in turn, depresses the average pay figures. Others argue that poorer educational qualifications and limited access to many occupations explain 75 per cent of the pay differentials. Still others believe that the differentials arise due to unequal work opportunities and demand pressure should be exerted to change the potent effects of covert and indirect discrimination.

In the meantime, some argue that the legislation will actually harm women. This is possible because employers may not consider women cost-efficient at the higher wages since they typically have lower levels of productivity, higher absenteeism due to the need to caretake for the family, and may take advantage of expensive maternity-leave provisions. The result may be that at a time of high unemployment, women are unloaded first and in greater numbers from the work force.

Equal pay and equal opportunities legislation may have their most positive long-term impacts through their tangential effects on the attempts made by younger women to gain education, experience and training. Changes in the law have signalled changing priorities and expectations, offering young women new goals. If this results in a better qualified and less hidebound woman, employers might be persuaded that women can also do the work.

In the long run, this will depend on what happens to women's roles in the family. As long as women divide their loyalties between a job and a family, they will be suspect as employees. The answer may be found in changing the domestic division of labour br by transforming the way employers attach value to their workers. Either way, the answer does not lie in current legislation.

The Meaning of Work

The growth of unemployment over recent years has led social scientists to consider the meaning of work on two fronts. First, they have asked what constitutes work. Secondly, they have asked what importance does work have in a person's life. It is worth considering these two areas in turn.

Any activity can be considered work. Sailing a boat can be a leisure pursuit or work. Welding two bits of metal together can be a hobby or work. Hitting a tennis ball can be a game or it can be work. It all depends on how the person doing it thinks about it: it is a subjective decision. One way around this definitional problem which has been proposed is that wé should distinguish between paid and unpaid work. Paid work, in an industrialised society, constitutes employment. The implication is that anything else is unemployment. Not surprisingly, many women, whose main work is domestic and unpaid, find this distinction irksome. They hardly consider themselves un-employed. They do work which needs to be done, and if they did not do it without payment, it would have to be done by someone else for payment. This is the logic of recent calls for wages for housework. Of course, this is where what starts as a semantic squabble becomes an economic issue focused upon who would have to pay.

The wages for housework campaign also reflects a concern about societal values. Women query whether their domestic work's worth is known or valued. Ironically, this doubt has grown with the development of the women's movement. The greater the challenge to the traditional female sex-role, the greater the pressure on women to re-evaluate their own lives and the more they doubt whether their domestic contribution is valued or, indeed, valuable. Many women who have devoted themselves totally to their family, home and community have found that their daughters denigrate their lives. They feel threatened by the new standards of behaviour expected of women. Threat triggers defensiveness and a rejection of new ways and different values, and a sort of entrenchment happens so that the value of staying at home and housework is overemphasised, becoming a central strut in the woman's self-definition.

Older women have this option of weaving a defensive cocoon about their lives. Younger ones have to face the challenge. The figures quoted earlier show that they do. At any one time, just under a third of women are out of paid work, but this is a changing population. The period spent out of work by any one woman is usually brief. For most women domestic work is the backdrop to paid employment. The value of housework then becomes important when its demands conflict with those of the occupation. Every day, women have to make decisions about where to pin their priorities: on housework or on their job. It is a worrying balancing act with no safety net. Errors lead to domestic strife or unemployment.

Researchers have assumed that for the majority of women unemployment carries none of the horrors it has for a man. Although the effects of unemployment are mediated by age, socio-economic class, geographical location, concomitant life events, and so on, the prime finding is that it constitutes a great trauma—for men. They become anxious, depressed, lose self-esteem, and are more subject to physical illness. For decades, there were no comparable studies of women who became unemployed. Folklore in the social sciences had it that women would cope better since they could withdraw into their domestic duties without substantial loss of social standing or financial penalty. Of course, this prediction was founded on the low-status, low-pay jobs most women were known to have. Strangely enough, the prediction is wrong. Recent work shows that women suffer just as much as men when they experience compulsory redundancy. Only women who voluntarily give up work for family reasons fare better.

Findings about the effects of unemployment on women serve to underline how important work is for women. Studies have shown that women are strongly 'work involved'. 'Work involvement' is an index of how much a person wishes to have a job and how central a place work holds in their life. Young women have been found to be more work involved than young men. Surveys of women's reasons for working have reaffirmed the importance it has for them. The majority of women work for financial reasons. They need the money for the family to be financially viable and to maintain their own autonomy. This contradicts a dominant notion that women work for pin-money that provides frills and fripperies and little luxuries. They also work often because of the intrinsic satisfaction they gain from doing the job, but this is definitely a secondary consideration to the financial imperative.

The criteria applied in choosing a job depend on whether the job is full- or part-time. Good pay and secure employment is the priority for full-time workers. Convenient hours is the prime consideration for the part-timer. Both emphasise that it has to be work that they like doing and the people have to be friendly to work with. Good promotion prospects are regarded as least important in choosing a job. It is important to stress that this is not because they would not take promotion were if offered, but rather because promotion prospects are so infrequently available that they are not a viable means of differentiating between jobs.

Women are spending a growing proportion of their lives in paid work. An average fifty-year-old now will have spent 60 per cent of her potential working life at work or actively seeking work; her daughter can expect to spend something like 75 per cent of hers at work. It is hardly surprising that, when asked, women claim that a woman's place is not in the home. They concede, however, that a woman with pre-school children should not work outside the home, even if they did so when their own children were young, but she should expect to return to work. Given these facts, the practical and psychological importance of work for women cannot be denied.

Intellectual Work

In describing the horizontal segregation of work earlier, there was an omission. Labour is not restricted to the hands, and products are not all material. The production of new ideas, whether in science or the arts, philosophy or social science, is also work. Ideas are valuable commodities, and traditionally women have not been noted for their contributions in these realms.

To some extent, this is because they have not attempted to contribute; largely because they have been forcibly excluded from education which might fit them for such work. However, some women have tried to become what Dale Spender has called 'Women of Ideas'. They are a minority, but it is startlingly clear that their ideas have not been promulgated and have often been actively subverted, trivialised, misrepresented or otherwise discredited. In her book, Spender catalogues women such as Aphra Behn, Mary Wollstonecraft, Angelina and Sarah Grimke, George Eliot, Dora Russell and others who contributed to the development of social understanding but whose work was, until recently, unrecognised. Spender argues effectively that this devaluation of women's intellectual work has been malicious and intentional, and that it is an ongoing process. The female intellectual is, after all, the antithesis of the proper woman.

Hiding from sight those women who succeed in developing new ideas has all sorts of advantages for a male-dominated society and intellectual establishment. Firstly, it is as if their aberrant behaviour and thought had never happened, so that no response or change is required. Secondly, such women are robbed of the social and academic power they might have justifiably expected. Thirdly, they cannot act as models for other women who might come later, which means that women intellectuals now have no notion of their gender's heritage. The deviants, though they spoke out often at great personal cost, have no continuing voice because publication, disciples and confirmation are denied them. They are now unearthed, weird archaeological specimens, by women who know they cannot possibly be the only women of ideas who have ever worked.

To claim that occupational segregation in this area is fading may be premature. It rather depends on how influential current female intellectuals are in the long run. Some of the evidence presented in the next chapter indicates the prospects may be gloomy.

Constructing an Identity for the Quiet Rebel

It is time now to draw a picture of the quiet rebel. Sleuth-like, from eye-witness statistics, an identikit can be put together. Each quiet rebel has a unique pattern of psychological and socio-economic characteristics, but they share their resistance to customary standards concerning women's work. Thus the commonalities in the profiles can be explored.

The quiet rebel can be found in types of work normally done by men: technical and scientific non-manual and skilled manual work. She will be found in high status jobs regardless of the type of work. She will be found isolated from other women, working in a sea of men. She will be found engaged in intellectual pursuits. She will be a full-time worker with young children in her care. Her earnings will be equivalent to her male counterparts'. Women in any of these situations can be called rebels. Some women will be rebels on several counts— possessing high status in a scientific job in the academic community and having young children, for instance, or gaining pre-eminence as a skilled craftsperson. The majority fail to conform in only one respect.

This socio-economic profile of the quiet rebel is culturally and temporally specific. It applies in the Western industrial-ised countries now. Historical period is vital in understanding the norms constraining women's work. In the past, even the recent past, women have been concentrated in skilled manual work or hauled into technical and scientific jobs during periods of national crisis. It is a tribute to convenience amnesia that these examples are not readily used to query women's sex roles now.

It is important to recognise that women who reject the limitations of women's work, although still in a minority, are by no means an insignificant minority. Yet they form no coherent group or movement and are unlikely to recognise that they have interests in common or share similar problems. The quiet rebel is not bounded by age, class, religion, or any other easily identifiable social label. There is thus no simple means of knowing one another. Any other woman in a crowd might be a quiet rebel. Before people can unite, they have to be able to recognise each other, and since recognition is a problem, unity is just a dream.

For some it would be a nightmare anyway. The quiet rebel resists the notion that she is politically militant. She may for that reason resist the one ideology or belief system that would cater for her needs directly: feminism.

Feminism is one of those chameleon words that has a different meaning for each hearer. Like all good ideologies, it offers a frame of reference for interpreting and explaining the state of the world. It explains that women's experience is determined by the control that men have of power in their societies. In addition, like all good ideologies, if offers a series of recipes for bringing about change. But also like all good ideologies, feminism has been plagued by schisms and sectarianism. Thus, within this broad feminist orientation there are a number of more or less radical and militant groups. The prescriptions for action differ, ranging from simple attempts to raise the consciousness of the woman in the street about her situation to suggestions that women should have no contact with men at all. The Women's Movement is what might be considered the political party which adheres to feminism, it is the practical arm of the doctrine. Undoubtedly, the Women's Movement, particularly in the United States, has been instrumental in bringing women together to act in a self-interested way as a political force. Much of the equal opportunities legislation was piloted by the Women's Movement. It would seem not only logical but inevitable that women resisting sex-role expectations at work would turn to feminism for sustenance and practical guidance. The fact that they most noticeably do not requires some explanation.

The message of feminism permeates to most women indirectly through the mass media. Consequently it reaches them pulped to a consistency most accessible to the lowest common denominator. A caricature of the feminist system of beliefs which exaggerates the extraordinary is paraded. Over the last decade, there is hardly another single group that has received as much negative coverage as the feminists. Feminist ideology has been set up as an Aunt Sally for any passing patriarch or chauvinist to throw at. A watered down, inconsistent version has been publicised, which anyone with a mind to destroy can do so at will. Women calling themselves feminists have been ridiculed and subjected to smear campaigns which challenge their right to be considered women. Their sexuality has been queried, their motives questioned, and their sanity denigrated. Social psychologists have found that a woman labelled feminist is immediately regarded as more aggressive, less attractive and less trustworthy than the same woman when not so labelled. Simply attaching the label transforms the way a woman is valued. Identifying oneself as a feminist is consequently a dangerous and risky business. It may be especially hazardous for a woman like our quiet rebel, who is already breaking custom and practice. Unless joining a feminist group can provide serious social support, the process of claiming to be a feminist can entail more costs than benefits.

The quiet rebel normally resorts to a compromise formulation. She will only admit herself a feminist if she can qualify it in some way which makes it clear that she is not militant, not active in the organisation, and not amenable to being caricatured. She may even believe that every woman is a feminist, but this merely symbolises how little she knows or cares about the principles underlying feminism. She believes in the clarion call for equality for women, but is just as likely to believe that men and women are 'equal but different'.

Basically, the mind of the quiet rebel is an ideological battlefield. She has few firm beliefs and no political stratagem. She holds simultaneously mutually incompatible beliefs: about the need for equality and the fact that it is already there; about the existence of discrimination and its prior eradication; about the value of militancy and its utter pointlessness. The whole realm of metatheory bemuses her. She cannot see its immediate relevance for her life and consequently feels it unnecessary to sort out what she personally really believes.

This picture of the quiet rebel should not be taken as an attempt to demean or berate her. The fact is that her confusion and lack of allegiance are justified. Feminism has not addressed itself to the majority of women in terms they can understand, and the representations of it which filter down through the press would confound a genius. Doubt and hesitancy are rational reactions.

Furthermore, feminism is class-based, and has been the preserve of educated, middle-class women. The quiet rebel can be found in all classes; but those from the working class would find many of the affluent assumptions of feminism hard to swallow. Of course, the spread of the quiet rebel across all classes serves to aggravate disunity and militates against corporate action.

The failure to coalesce around a common goal or ideology has two consequences: firstly, the quiet rebel remains isolated, dealing with problems on an individual basis; and secondly, she remains truly 'quiet' because she has no one to give voice to her views at a national level. This issue of gaining a voice and being heard is something which is re-examined in later chapters. The point about the difficulty of dealing with problems individually is more immediately salient.

Difficulties manifested by the quiet rebel take many forms: conflict with workmates, trauma in the family, psychological stress and physical illnesses are a small selection. However, these difficulties have a common root. These women are challenging the rules; in doing so, they threaten both their own identity and that of those around them. They shake the stability of the system.

The notion of identity is very important. A person's identity has two components: self-definition and self-esteem. Self-definition is concerned with how a person describes herself; it is a kind of contents checklist. So someone might describe herself as fat, fair and forty, and subject to gallstones. Self-esteem is concerned with how the person values or gains satisfaction from the contents of her identity. Being fat might be a real pain, being forty a considerable blessing. How a person describes herself and proceeds to value herself is highly dependent upon other people and society's standards. A woman might not consider herself fat until she is told by a next-door neighbour; she might not feel it is bad to be fat until she is told by her doctor.

Occupational category clearly contributes to the components of self-definition. A woman breaking with sex-role expectations is likely to incur displeasure from various influential sources who will make it clear that the contribution of her job to her identity is incompatible with other elements in it and should not be positively valued. The quiet rebel may persist in valuing that component of her self-definition, but the nagging challenge to her own appraisal will remain. It will continue as a threat to the stability of her identity.

To the extent that she lives with the threat to her identity, each quiet rebel shares a common set of psychological dynamics. Each will try to fend off the threat to her self-definition and self-esteem and at the same time seek to repair damages sustained. There are standard tactics people can use in coping with threat. Some employ them automatically, others can be educated to use them. One of the aims of this book is to describe these techniques for the management of threat. In some ways, it is thus a self-help manual for the quiet rebel. The groundwork for self-defence begins in the next chapter with the maxim 'know your enemy'. It outlines the barriers which lie in the path of the quiet rebel; barriers which could prevent the potential rebel from ever breaking with tradition and gaining men's work. Dismantling barriers, or, if that fails, scaling them, is something which requires much thought and skill.

Further Reading

Burman, S. (ed.), *Fit Work for Women*. London: Croom Helm, 1979.
Spender, D., *Women of Ideas*. London: ARK, 1982.

Hoiberg, A. (ed.), *Women and the World of Work*. New York: Plenum, 1982.

Martin, J. and Roberts, C., *Women and Employment: A Lifetime Perspective*. London: HMSO, 1984.

Radcliffe Richards, J., *The Sceptical Feminist*. London: Routledge and Kegan Paul, 1980.

Hakim, C., *Occupational Segregation: A Comparative Study of the Degree and Pattern of Men and Women's Work in Britain, the US and Other Countries*. Research Paper No. 9, Dept of Employment, HMSO, 1979.

Meehan, E.M., *Women's Rights at Work: Campaigns and Policy in Britain and the United States*. London: MacMillan, 1985.

Chapter Two
BREAKING IN

The barriers facing the quiet rebel are by no means all external and material. Some of them she will have internalised, assimilating them so that they form part of her character and channel the way she thinks. An understanding of how this process of internalisation occurs is fundamental to any explanation of what barriers there are and how they function.

Stereotyping Womanhood

The central barrier, and one which shapes and fuels the rest, is the stereotype of women which permeates society. Stereotype is a word which is commonly used and equally commonly misused and misunderstood. Properly speaking, a stereotype is a syndrome of characteristics attributed to a group of people; every member of that group is then expected to possess those characteristics. The normal format goes: 'all so and sos are such and such'. For instance, 'all redheads are fiery-tempered'; 'all Scots are mean'; 'all fat people are sociable'. If a person holds a stereotype of a group or category, she or he expects any member of that group to possess the stereotypic qualities. Stereotypes also normally specify the value of the characteristics concerned: their temper is attractive; their meanness laughable; their sociability pitiable.

Stereotypes can take a tenacious hold on the imagination, largely because they are useful tools and make life easy. You meet a new person, you establish to which group they belong, and you think you know what and who they are. Stereotypes short-cut the laborious business of really getting to know other people. More important, perhaps, stereotypes are useful weapons in rivalries between groups. Groups, whenever they can, create deprecating stereotypes of their enemies: they are wicked, stupid, corrupt, and so on. In this way, the stereotype justifies hostility against them, and can even legitimate their subjection or annihilation. Stereotypes de-individualise opponents, deprive them of their uniqueness and make them less like oneself, bringing treatment of them which evades the constraints that would limit abuse of others similar to oneself one step closer.

It is important to recognise that stereotypes serve their functions whether they are accurate or not. The stereotype of a group does not have to reveal the truth about it. By definition, the application of a stereotype has to be full of error, since it denies people their basic uniqueness. Evidence of the in-accuracies of a stereotype tend to be ignored, and maintaining a stereotype in the face of contradictory facts is commonplace. The functional value of a stereotype is too great for it to be abandoned, and the struggle to hold on to a stereotype often involves fascinating mental contortions. For instance, someone might hold the stereotype that all feminists are unattractive and aggressive, but she knows Beth who is a feminist, attractive *and* pacific. In that sort of situation, Beth's membership of the stereotyped group is often challenged: she cannot *really* be a feminist. In fact, Beth's friend is turning a blind eye to one of her defining characteristics, and the stereotype and the friend-ship are maintained intact so long as Beth does not set about proving that she *is* a feminist.

Stereotypes arise in the first place through the attempts of groups to establish an identity for themselves and to impose less advantageous identities on other groups. The power a group has is closely tied to its stereotype, and the more power it has, the more likely it is to be able to dictate its own stereotype and those of other groups. Clearly, effective manipulation of the stereotype can in the long run enhance the group's power; it can emphasise its moral, intellectual and material superiority over rivals. Since stereotypes tend to be believed, this can be rather daunting to anybody daring to challenge a powerful group.

Many social scientists believe that stereotypes act as self-fulfilling prophesies: a group stereotyped as brave, ambitious and dominating becomes such, and acts out the predictions embodied in the stereotype. Why should this be so? Probably because humans are conformist creatures, who like to do what is expected of them. Of course, the conformity is supported by a system of rewards and punishments. The closer your life approximates to the ideal, the greater your emotional and material rewards. Those who control the rewards have the power to fulfil their own prophesies. This explains why in some cases people comply with stereotypes that demean and virtually dehumanise them: failure to do so is too punishing.

This excursion into the dynamics of stereotyping is a necessary precursor to a consideration of the stereotyping of womanhood. For the purposes of stereotyping, women as a whole are treated as a homogeneous group, or, if you bridle at the term group, as a social category. This is problematic, of course, since women can be divided by age, race, class, religion, culture, marital status, work, and whatever other dimension of social differentiation one cares to mention. The stereotype rides roughshod over such trivia: women are united by their womanhood and this is all it cares about.

The stereotype says women are: emotional, passive, nurturant, weak, dependent, decorative, non-assertive, and incompetent except in narrowly defined domestic chores. This is the stereotype of what is often called the 'traditional woman'.

Men, in contrast, are almost the polar opposite: active, dominating, unemotional, technically competent, exploitative, ambitious, and independent.

The 'traditional woman' and 'traditional man' are both, in essence, one-dimensional. Women are archetypally 'expressive', which is meant to connote emotionality and spontaneity without rational calculation in the pursuit of self-interests; the emphasis is upon servicing others, because personal relationships are more important than anything else. Men are 'instrumental' in orientation: strength, aggression, and relationships are used as a means to other ends; everything is a move in the great plan to maximise self-gain.

Few people, male or female, would recognise themselves in these 'ideal types', and all the evidence supports this rejection. Psychologists have found *no evidence* of the proposed differences between the sexes in relation to levels of competitiveness, dominance, nurturance, suggestibility, sociability, activity or desire for achievement. They have found *no differences* in anxiety levels, cognitive or analytic abilities, or amounts of self-esteem.

There are small differences in average levels of aggression: men are on average more aggressive, but there is tremendous overlap of scores, with many women just as aggressive as men. On tests of verbal abilities (spelling, writing and comprehension of texts), women on average score better than men, but the difference is slight and again there is a wide overlap of the sexes. Men perform marginally better on average on spatial (for instance, recognising how jumbled figures should be reconstituted) and mathematical tests, but again the overlap of scores is marked. The repetition of 'on average' and 'overlap' is not accidental. They emphasise that the sex of a person does not predict their abilities. On average women may be less aggressive, but a large minority of women are more or equally as aggressive as their male counterparts. With such a spread of scores, averages say little about individuals.

If any attention were paid to the bulk of the evidence, the

stereotypes would shrivel. They do not do so because they serve a valuable purpose. The stereotypes reify the gulf between men and women; they glory in the dualism between 'expressive' and 'instrumental'. But they go further: women are not only different, they are worse. The characteristics attributed to women are not as socially valued as those allotted to men. The male stereotype is tied to male dominance and power and thus takes on the value inherent in the possession of power. The stereotyping of womanhood over the centuries can be taken as an exemplar of how a group with power will distinguish itself maximally from those it subjugates and in a manner which incapacitates them. Women characterised as passive, non-aggressive, dependent and nurturant, once they assimilate that self-image, are unlikely to unite in attempts to grasp power.

Of course, the system of attaching value to the stereotype is neither as simple nor as overt as that. If it were, it would be visible and unconvincing. In fact, the powerplay tactics have a sugar-sweet backup. While the female stereotype has low social value, the women who conformed to it, traditionally, have been given considerable social value. It is like being rewarded for being best at being second-best. The result is that it is all too easy to confuse the value of the stereotype itself with the value of conforming to it.

It is interesting that, in tackling the stereotype of woman-hood, feminists have taken two quite contradictory approaches. Some have argued that women should abandon the 'expressive' mould and, instead, adopt an 'instrumental' orientation. Supporters of this have a tendency to say that women should reject their previous selves. Others call for the reverse: women should deify their 'expressive' selves and work for them to be credited with social value and respect. Both are suggestive and respectable forms of attack against the stereo-type. Unfortunately, both make the fundamental error of treating the stereotype as if it reflected the truth about women. The most potent attack against the stereotype will have to include attempts to make people realise that it is not accurate. It is only by proving that men and women are not uni-dimensional that their treatment will be changed. All that is known about the tenacity of stereotypes would imply that such a change of consciousness is not easily attained. Objective proof is a weak weapon where people are capable of such feats of mental gymnastics as those that permit whole systems of knowledge to be dismissed or trivialised.

Stereotyping also includes built-in self-defence mechanisms. Stereotypes are not static; they evolve as necessary over time with the inclusion of new characteristics to be attributed to the group. Sometimes this results in a list of mutually exclusive attributes. For instance, during the time of their enslavement in the United States, blacks were simultaneously considered loyal, stupid and cunningly quick witted. This over-inclusive-ness means that it is difficult to evade the prescriptions of the stereotype completely; it traps you whichever way you turn. Proving it fallacious is a problem. The second automatic defence reaction of the stereotype is evinced in its ability to tolerate exceptions to its rule by excluding the exception from the group. A woman who does not comply with the stereotype is no real woman: her sexual identity is suspect. She is relegated into a sub-class of the genus woman which is catered for by its own stereotype. For instance, the 'feminist woman' is subjected to just as virulent a stereotype as the 'traditional woman'. Once the eviction has been completed, the stereotype is safe again.

The quiet rebel, in her struggle to gain 'men's work', will face the full frontal force of the stereotypes. Possession of the characteristics specified in the male stereotype is normally assumed necessary to gain 'men's work'. The quiet rebel will be assumed to conform to the female stereotype and be assumed unsuited to such work. All of these assumptions may be invalid, but they guide action: both that of the potential rebel and that of her potential employer.

The quiet rebel must self-consciously reject the stereotype of womanhood. The fact that she contemplates rebellion in the first place indicates that she has assimilated that stereotypic self-image incompletely. However, there is a world of difference between feeling ill at ease with the stereotype and abandoning it. Unease with the stereotype may have arisen from various roots: in the family, at school, or through the influence of world-wide events represented in the media. Some of the reasons for wishing to rebel are considered later in the book; at issue here is how the stereotype can be countered.

Resisting the Stereotype

There may be little the individual quiet rebel can do to counter the stereotype. Her resistance, at least initially, has to be personal. It takes place at a cognitive level, inside her head, in thought and feeling. She has to change herself by changing the way she thinks. There seem to be four stages in this process:

1. Recognising the stereotype for what it is—a malicious fiction probably not applicable to any real, live woman and certainly inapplicable to herself.

2. Recognising that the stereotype is designed to make one feel guilty for failure to live up to its 'ideal woman' and rejecting that guilt.

3. Recognising that rejection of the stereotype will result in self-doubt and that this is disarming and pointless.

4. Recognising there are other women doing the same, or very similar, things and using them as models for an alternative picture of successful womanhood.

This process of reconceptualisation will not prevent others

from attacking the woman who deviates severely from the stereotype, but it is a starting point in tackling the internalised barriers against the quiet rebellion. You, yourself, have to believe the stereotype is wrong, and wrong in all respects, factually and morally, before you can convince others.

Permissible Roles for Women

The stereotype of womanhood acts in collusion with a system of role prescriptions. A role is both a social position and the set of behaviours expected of someone in that position. It parallels the idea of a role in a theatrical production: the person portraying a specific role has certain actions and utterances to make. Different cultures have contributed a whole galaxy of roles for women to occupy. Anthropologists have labelled only some: the Mother (ubiquitous it seems), the Virgin, the Witch, the Whore, the Amazon, the Bitch, and, latterly, the Feminist. Each are represented by stereotypes which act as almost subordinate clauses to the central stereotype of womanhood. Each is like a one-sided, cardboard cutout, reminiscent of figures in pulp drama or TV soap operas (or maybe it works the other way round). They represent shards of a real identity, fixed in aspic in order to stand alone.

The problem is that there is a societal conspiracy to perpetuate typecasting. We all like to plunge others irremediably into a single role. Having established oneself as the Virgin, it is possible to have great fun making the arduous transition to the Whore. We may cosset fixed notions of others' roles, but each of us in our private mind games, played in the imaginary world of wish-fulfilment, garb ourselves kaleidoscopically in novel roles. In the dark recesses of her head, what wonderful Mother has not become a ball-breaking man-eating, Machiavellian Bitch?

In examining the roles, it is clear that each focuses upon a different aspect of a woman's sexuality: one subordinates it to reproduction, one treats it as wickedness incarnate, one suggests it is icy manipulation, and one even hints at its total absence. It is an interesting exercise to estimate how far each depends on the image of woman as a sexual creature. There seems to be a clear dichotomy: she is either totally so or not at all, no happy medium allowed.

None of the roles are work roles—with the possible exception of the Whore, but this normally connotes no dedication to prostitution as a trade. None carry prescriptions about work outside the home; they carry many, of course, about work inside the home. Nevertheless, when women move into paid employment they import these role preconceptions. What typing pool does not have its Mother to whom everyone can turn in crisis or dismay? What production-line does not have its very own Bitch, ever ready with the put-down, always with an eye for the cute angle? What health-care unit does not stand in awe of the purity and untouchable innocence of its resident Virgin?

The quiet rebel is by no means immune from such type-casting. In fact, her presence in 'men's work' serves to accentuate its likelihood. She is, after all, probably the only woman around doing that work and, consequently, the only candidate available to perform the roles. Of course, macho mythology, because she is doing what women do not normally do, may prefer to cast her in some roles rather than others. The Amazon, the Bitch, the Feminist are all favourites, because they both partially explain her presence in a man's job and carry pejorative overtones. Perhaps more surprisingly, she may also be treated as the Witch. This characterisation often occurs when a woman gains power and promotion, and it is largely used by those men she has beaten in competition. It is as though witchcraft is the only thing that can explain her success. Almost incidentally, it acts as a put-down: witches are too frequently old harridans for it to be anything else.

It is fascinating how frequently women who are successful in male-dominated industries, and who consequently gain power which is rarely found in the hands of a woman, are regarded as Bitches and Witches. It is exceedingly rare that they are genuinely praised as talented or determined, and even rarer that they are recognised as 'good fellows' in the sense of having an admirable character or demeanour. It is almost as if men think a woman must be corrupt to get power, and more corrupted by it once she has it. Moreover, they are not the grand misdeeds that can be confused with enthusiasm for an ideal; powerful women are troubled, according to the myth, with petty corruptions: small-minded, short-sighted malicious-ness and ignorance. The Bitch and Witch roles are erected to question the woman's entitlement to the job and her motives in performing tasks essential to it. They enable every action to be interpreted in the worst possible light. The role offered the woman deprives her success and power of much of its flavour.

The quiet rebel being pushed into role conformity has a number of options open to her. She can capitulate and *act out* the role, fulfilling all its prescriptions plus some: Superbitch is born. There is a lot to be said for this, as long as the role is fundamentally amenable to the individual woman. For instance, it means that she puts on a mask while at work that can come to be an armour. Her real self sits quietly beneath. Acting out the role may mean she is less attacked, because she is at least conforming in some respects to what is expected of her as a woman. There are, however, potential hazards in adopting this strategy: the mask may get stuck. Removing the role may be very difficult, and it may transfer disastrously to the domestic sphere.

Clare, a woman in her late thirties who had made it to the top in the sales section of a large computer business, typifies this problem. The men with whom Clare worked attributed to her the Superbitch image and, in time, she 'grew into' it. The problem lay in dropping it with her husband and family. Being sharp-tongued, aggressive and exploitative 9 till 5 does not make it easy to be a nurturant, selfless listener in the evening. She discovered she was becoming the cardboard cutout. She was impatient with indecision, expected promises to have things done to be kept religiously, and failed to understand that her unrelenting pressure was leading everyone to feel overstressed. She was using the same managerial tactics at home that she found effective at work. Just as at work she would never allow anyone to get the better of her, so at home she had to win any disagreement or squabble, and her methods were not always very savoury. But then she had the chance to stop and look at herself at a time when her husband fell ill, and she decided that this was not really her; she knew her own personality was being swamped by her work persona. The mask she wore to work was taking over. Over the next few months, she made a conscious effort to break the mould at home: she stopped trying to 'win' at all costs. Strangely, she found that her changed attitude at home spread to the office. She started to listen more and relax a mite. This made her less predictable to colleagues and actually benefited her, since she maintained her competence in the job while reducing her overt aggression. She still had problems after particularly fraught days in unwinding after work, but she identified this as a problem and actually took time before leaving for home to 'settle her mind and her emotions'. She had concluded that she did not really need the mask at home or at work, but knew that it was always there to be repositioned should the occasion arise.

In cases like Clare's, the role cages the woman until she finds the key to unlock its door. Yet sometimes it is not the woman who is responsible for exporting the work role to life outside. Often men carry their preconceptions about powerful women into their social lives. They assume that the woman will be unable to drop the work role and treat her accordingly. The woman faced with that has to begin the battles so familiar at work during her leisure time, or capitulate and act out the role again. The catalogue is endless of examples of women who will not tell new men they meet about their work because they are sick to death of being typecast. Sophie, aged twenty-eight, the personnel director of a chain of electronics companies with a staff of over fifty for whom she is responsible, claims to be a personnel secretary when meeting people casually at parties because she finds if she tells the truth she scares men away. She says they assume she will be the hard, ambitious, ruthless type that she knows she is not.

Men find it difficult to believe that a woman who is powerful at work can drop the trappings of her role when she is away from work. To the extent that they show this to the women themselves, they create the very behaviour they expect. The women fulfil the men's prophecy and act out their worst fears. Men who do this create their own monsters.

Some quiet rebels take a completely opposite path to acting out from the start. They insist on being their 'real selves'. This is very hard on the self-concept. Rejecting the roles means going further down the road to the total refutation of idealised womanhood, and it takes a strong woman to do that. Most often the attempt is subverted anyway, because whatever she does to be uniquely herself, the quiet rebel is pigeonholed by those with whom she works.

Some women, faced with the typecasting difficulty, resort to attempts to deny their sexuality and take elaborate steps to neuter themselves metaphorically. Their clothes, their cosmetics, their hairdo, their mode of speech, even their way of walking and sitting, are tailored to make their femininity minimally noticeable. It can never be magicked away, but it is not blatant. They treat their sex as if it were irrelevant and encourage others to do the same. This is a ploy which can gain transient success, but its long-term viability is tenuous: gender role typecasting is too ingrained a preoccupation of the majority for a woman to be able to fool all of the people, all of the time.

Neutering oneself is an option less frequently chosen nowadays than it used to be. Women now in their late fifties often claim that they had to do it to survive when they started on their long trek to career success in banking, insurance, publishing, or whatever. Sarah, currently executive director of a pharmaceutical firm, at fifty-nine looks back with grim humour at her own efforts to neuter herself. In her twenties she remembers how she tried to 'blend into the wallpaper and office or laboratory furniture' so as not to attract attention to herself. She wore severe tailored suits that echoed those of the men around her. Her makeup was subdued and designed to give the impression that she 'was making an effort without trying to attract'. Sarah has survived and prospered in her work despite a series of trauma in her industry and now feels free to express her feminity in adornment and physical presentation. Nevertheless, she is still hyperalert to the dangers of placing her sexuality to the fore in her job. Now she feels protected by the march of time; age, she says, has its advantages: friendliness is rarely now misconstrued as flirtation, and her idiosyncracies of dress are accepted as expressions of her personality not her sexuality. Yet she is keen to point out that 'neutering' oneself goes further than altering one's clothes or abandoning an exotic perfume. Neutering has to occur at the emotional level too. Women symbolise their sex by their emotionality and sensitivity, or so the myth has it. Neutering oneself means silencing emotions and empathy lest they be treated as expressions of the female spirit. Sarah argues that this, for her, has always been the hardest hurdle. She talks about 'chopping off a part of one's humanity to look like the business image of the great male god'. Women who become emotional neuters at work are, in a sense, likely to appear the typical Bitch. We come full cycle: seeking to evade the role, the woman runs headlong into it.

As far as gender roles are concerned, for the quiet rebel it seems to be a case of heads you lose, tails you lose. Conformity with them warps your identity; resistance to them may be personally satisfying but externally futile, because you cannot control how others persist in perceiving you. One way to go beyond the toss of the coin may be self-consciously to manipulate role occupancy. This would entail shifting from one role to the next in a way which suited one's self-interest: being the Bitch, the Whore, the Mother at times which were most likely to benefit oneself. This strategy has a series of advantages. Regular changes mean it is unlikely you confuse the role for your real self. To some extent, you are feeding people what they want, fulfilling their expectations but not in their interests. You thus capitalise upon their preconceptions because you know the emotions each role precipitates in others: the Mother, dependence and truculent obedience; the Bitch, envy and fear; and so on. Acting the role can mean that after a while you are able to manipulate these feelings skilfully.

Joanna, a civil engineer by training who works as a building surveyor in a construction company, uses this 'mix and match' tactic. She claims to know when to don the character of the Bitch and the ways of the Mother, and with whom. She also uses what she calls her 'Big Sister Act'. She uses this with men working for her who are roughly the same age or younger. By emphasising that she knows more than they do but will use her experience for their mutual benefit in getting the job done, she finds that she can avoid being regarded as a powercrazy Bitch and can gain their cooperation. 'Big Sister', Joanna states, is trustworthy and very definitely in charge; she also precludes any sexual advances getting in the way of business because they smack too much of incest with such a persona. The point to emphasise about Joanna is that she chooses which role to enact depending upon the circumstances. She is not pushed into a characterisation which is disadvantageous to herself. Joanna manipulates her role performance, shifting from one to another with practiced ease and coordinating them just as she might match coordinates in her wardrobe.

Manipulating roles means shifting from being the passive

recipient of roles which are imposed to being an active determiner of the composite picture of oneself. Admittedly, initially, the choice is limited by the range of roles available. Ultimately, however, one can envisage that the quiet rebel, by adopting this strategy, could create a new archetypal role for women at work which encompasses facets of the old ones plus distinctive features of its own, like competence and skill.

Women who choose to stay outside established roles will generate this new archetypal role. Their behaviour, emotions and thoughts will be seen as characterising a new sort of woman at work in male-dominated professions, one who encompasses the most effective elements of the previous roles (the sensitivity of the Mother without her passivity; the assertiveness of the Bitch without her maliciousness; the magic of the Witch without her fearsomeness), but who has more. She will have recognised talent and be respected. Building into the role the notion that a woman doing a 'man's job' can be good at it without trickery or deceit will be a new departure. As more women show this to be the case, the transformation of role prescriptions will come. It will mean that young women entering such work will have a new role to model themselves upon and it will be interesting to see whether the new role will remain free of the negative overtones so redolent of existing roles. It will be unlikely to do so, since anyone who dislikes women doing men's work will try to smear it with the pejorative connotations now associated with the other roles. It is possible to envisage that the new role of 'Effective Worker' will soon show signs of cracking under the burden of snide asides. Yet this is not too worrying. The important point is that the quiet rebel should know that roles are not immutable; they do evolve, and there is no reason for a determined woman to stick to a role which she detests. The quiet rebel has consciously to manipulate and create her role at work.

Childhood Ideas about Work

Stereotypes and role prescriptions are barriers the quiet rebel can overcome, if at considerable cost. There is a second sort of barrier more immediately relevant to work: the ideas she has learnt about work as a child. Children as young as four years of age are able to state what sort of work a man should do and what sort a woman should do, and the younger the child, the more categorical and dogmatic the dichotomy. For young children, the division is unquestionable, and it is almost wicked to challenge it.

Their system of beliefs is actually quite complicated. When asked why men and women do different jobs, they answer that men are strong and women have babies and that is why. If asked whether women and men could do particular jobs (e.g. car mechanic, shop assistant, hairdresser), they agree that they could do them equally well. But they are quick to point out that they ought not to swop jobs. Women in men's jobs and vice versa are not seen as such attractive or good people as those who abide by the rules.

What are seen as men's jobs and women's jobs differ across cultures. The classic, much criticised study of the natives of Papua, New Guinea, by Margaret Mead in the 1950s showed that there women had responsibility for the hunting, fishing, and fighting jobs and men the domestic chores. Children there treated those allocations as immutably fixed, too. Children learn what to think right and wrong, and what to expect from adults and other older children. They consequently echo societal rules in the most pointed and obvious ways.

Children of all cultures explain the sexual division of labour in biological terms: strength, reproductive functions, etc. A biological explanation gives staunch support to the *status quo*, whatever the *status quo* happens to be. A biological explanation implies the present arrangements are natural, inevitable, and unchangeable. The nature-nurture debate is as old as the rejection of religion. On the nature side, there is the argument that sex differences are caused by different genetic endowments. On the nurture side, there is the argument that they are bought about by differential patterns of child-rearing. Put crudely, girls will be girls because of their chromosomes, versus girls will be girls because of their dollies, dresses and delicate treatment. In truth, the polarisation is artificial and misleading. No characteristic, physical or psychological, is produced solely by either heredity or environment. From the moment of conception in the environment of the womb, both act in concert to create the finished product. Yet the persistence of the purely biological explanation is strong. Its recent resurgence includes theories focusing upon the operation of sex hormones, differential brain development, and natural selection processes during hominid evolution (the core of sociobiology). For some, the attraction of the biological explanation can be seen in its support of the status quo. For others, the majority, its beauty lies in its simplicity. It is accepted because it is easy to understand. What is easier than saying some people are aggressive because it is instinctive? As long as you do not question too closely what instinct might be, the explanation is complete. It is certainly so seamless in its tautology that the alternative multifactorial explanation seems messy and unsatisfactory by comparison, because it has to say that many things make a person aggressive and they do not do it consistently nor do they operate alone. The child absorbs the simpler rationalisation.

The result is that children grow up with fixed ideas about the value of and reasons for the sexual division of labour in and outside the home. These ideas are learnt, as the cross-cultural comparisons show. They can consequently be unlearnt. There is evidence that this happens: older children have a less strict adherence to the dichotomy. They recognise people can and do break the barrier, but only a small minority say that they would be willing to do so. The majority of teenagers will pick jobs which are 'appropriate' for their gender and regard anyone who does not as suspect. Not surprisingly, the more highly qualified a young woman is academically, the more likely she is to consider men's work appropriate for her. This is possibly because she is looking for high status work with good prospects, since this is most often men's work, and the odds are that she will decide to ignore gender prescriptions. She does this, however, in full knowledge of them.

Childhood ideas about work linger, and the quiet rebel has to overcome the barrier they represent. They are consumed with one's mother's milk, and abandoning the model for behaviour which she provided is traumatic. Children model themselves upon, emulate, the people who are significant in their lives. Time and again, it is found that women who themselves take men's jobs have mothers, or central female figures in their lives, who had also done so. We all copy our elders and betters. In changing children's ideas of the sexual division of labour, it is important that adequate models are available. The quiet rebel can best help herself by ensuring that she chooses the right model to copy. This may mean consciously choosing to desert old idols.

Recognising the fallacy of the purely biological explanation of so-called sex differences, and accepting the fact that ideas about the division of labour by gender are learnt not instinctual, are important steps for the quiet rebel. They are as important as realising that most sex differences are fictional products of stereotyping. The quiet rebel cuts the ties to childhood in treading these steps.

The Impact of Education

The impact of the education system has been a major barrier to women moving into men's work, since schools have reinforced the sexual division of labor with all their considerable

might. They work at two levels: through the official curriculum and the hidden curriculum. Until 1972, with the passage
of Title IX (of the Education Amendments) which forbids all
forms of sex-based discrimination in educational institutions,
schools could arrange tracking systems so that it was virtually
impossible for girls to study 'boys' subjects'. A national survey
conducted in 1972 showed that 95 per cent of all agriculture
course students were male, 93 per cent of those studying
consumer and homemaking courses were female, 92 per cent
registered in technical courses, *e.g.* metallurgy, engineering,
oceanography, were male, 75 per cent in office skills courses
were female. The segregation even extended to type of sport
played. In 1971, boys' participation in high school sports was
12 times that of girls.

The legislation has meant that overt funnelling of school-
children has declined and there is now a legal obligation to
offer equal education to all children. It is too early to make
conclusions about the impact this may have. In any case, its
impact is likely to be minimised by the operation of the hidden
curriculum.

The hidden curriculum is the label given to the ambience,
attitudes and patterns of interaction in a school, and it is
argued by many educationalists that the hidden curriculum
still supports the traditional notions of the girl and boy pupil.
Girls are denied models of successful female academics in
their teachers because women do not gain promotions in
teaching anywhere near proportionally to their numbers. They
congregate in the lower status institutions and less esteemed
subject areas. The majority of elementary teachers are female:
85 per cent in 1975 and this figure has been roughly stable
over 15 years. The majority of principals and administrators
are male. Female teachers predominate in the early post-
elementary years when subject matter is relatively simple,
prestige mediocre and salary insubstantial. Male teachers are
most prevalent in the later years when prestige and salary
increase. In 1977 half of high school teachers were male, 70–

80 per cent of college teachers were male. Similarly, a disproportionate number of men teach in universities and more of them gain full professorships. Despite affirmative action, these patterns have hardly altered since 1972. The average student is continually confronted with wildly disparate role models for males and females in the education system. This is part of the hidden curriculum: covert lessons to be learnt at school.

Teachers differ in their attitudes and overt behaviour towards boys and girls. They expect less of girls intellectually, do not drive them so hard, and offer them less stringent or demanding tasks. This is echoed in interaction patterns. Teachers, of both sexes, spend more time interacting with the boys. Observation studies in classrooms in the US and Europe have shown that although boys bear the brunt of teacher disapproval and critical attention, they also receive the greater part of their approval and encouragement. Girls, regardless of their behaviour, receive less feedback. More importantly, the positive attention they receive supports passivity. Disruptive, active, or inquisitive boys are reinforced by the amount of attention devoted to them. Girls who behave in this way are more likely to be ignored. The system acts to perpetuate a dichotomy in response patterns. In addition, textbooks and reading books used extensively in schools have been repeatedly shown to characterise men and women in terms of the conventional stereotypes. All these components of the hidden curriculum reaffirm the inequality of the sexes and militate against girls' academic success or their pursuit of 'masculine' subjects.

The effectiveness of the hidden curriculum is reflected not only in the ratio of boys to girls taking science and technical subjects at school. The effects on the academic aspirations of women are seen in the fact that far fewer women seek to pursue a higher education. Women going to university or college congregate in 'female' subjects (language and literature courses). In 1979, the National Center for Education

Statistics published the figures for the percentage of women among bachelor's degree recipients in science and engineering for the period 1971 to 1978. In mathematics in 1971 the percentage was 39.1; by 1978 it was 41.3. In computer science, the comparable figures are 13.6 and 25.8. There was a marked increase in the physical sciences, too, 15.1 to 25.5. The increase was even greater in agriculture, 5.5 to 24.6, and in engineering there was an increase of 1 per cent to 6.7 per cent. Of course, despite these increases, the absolute number of women in these disciplines is small compared with the biological and social sciences where they represent about 40 per cent of the students.

On graduation, women go into public services and education, rather than commerce and industry. Men do the reverse. In the US, women graduating in science or engineering are just as likely to go on to take a higher degree as men. Often they complete their doctorate faster, work in equally prestigious university departments, and are just as likely to gain a job on completion. In the US, women form 10 per cent of the doctoral labor force in science and engineering. However, they have been largely employed in the universities, not commerce, and tend to be paid less and remain in low status positions longer than men of equal experience and qualifications. Affirmative action may be changing this pattern now, since in the last five years the number of women taking engineering degrees has doubled. Changes in social attitudes in the US are permitting women to shift into 'male' academic subjects, and they do so to great effect. The idea that women have some inbuilt block against science and technology is bunk, an old husband's tale told to keep the quiet rebel quiet.

For the quiet rebel who has left school with non-scientific, non-technical qualifications, the transition into men's work can be hard. Most professional and craft training requires a minimum level of scientific or technical qualification. However, when women are given access to such training, even though they do not possess the normally stipulated background, they can succeed well. As long as their training allows them to catch up on what they have missed, and this is rarely time consuming since they are highly motivated, they do just as well as those with prior qualifications. This finding has implications for employers as well as for the women themselves. Employers may get a very good deal from a highly motivated female trainee despite previous ignorance. Women should accept the fact that school successes or failures are not a life-time's ball-and-chain.

The fears and failures of women at school are largely a product of the educational system, and this needs to be changed for future generations of women. For those women already harmed by it, re-education is vital. Moreover, it is available if they choose to seek it out. The quiet rebel has to re-educate herself in many realms; forgetting the intellectual horrors engendered in her by school is one.

The Selection Procedure

The most immediate barrier to the quiet rebel gaining men's work is presented by the prejudices of careers guidance and personnel managers, who turn young women off countless jobs. Surveys of supposedly enlightened careers counsellors show that neither male nor female counsellors approved of non-typical careers choices. They focus their counselling upon attempts to change the client's choice. They offer no information on the job required, warn of the extreme difficulties of such work for a woman, and reiterate the sex-specific stereotypes attached to the job. So, for example, engineering is damned as dirty, manual, hard to get, shift-work, overtime, and so on. Several measures used to assess vocational interest are inherently biased: the female version of the questionnaires omits occupations and interests stereotypically masculine.

Careers brochures echo sex stereotypes subtly in the examples and illustrations chosen. Women are pictured doing the servicing jobs, men taking the decisions. It is worth acknowledging that there is no sexual discrimination involved in the application of these biases. Young men desiring women's work are equally subject to misinformation and conformity pressures.

Careers advice offered to young people is designed to bolster the sexual division of labour, and it affects them at a time when they are particularly vulnerable. They are vulnerable because they may be almost totally ignorant of the job they think they might like, and because they may be unsure about whether they really want it. Information given at such a time which feeds their doubt or fear is bound to dissuade them. Furthermore, vulnerability leads to susceptibility. A young woman walking into a careers office may want to be a TV lighting technician; having been told about the fierce competition for such jobs, the closed shop, the technical and scientific background requirements, when it is suggested to her that she might alternatively like to be a production secretary in the same industry, she is prepared for suggestibility. Supplanting realistic ambitions for impossible ones is the task of careers guidance. However, this can be carried too far. Careers guidance has been used to perpetuate barriers to women entering certain avenues of employment by redirecting the ambitions which young women have for their future.

The reasons for the persistence of such biases in careers guidance services are twofold. Firstly, bureaucratic inertia works against change, especially since once young people leave school in Britain much counselling is left in the hands of untrained employment assistants. Secondly, and more importantly, the guidance services actually have two clients: the person looking for work and the employers. Keeping employers satisfied may mean keeping the job-seeker dissatisfied. But the services are dependent on employers using them, 'giving them vacancies', and so they cannot afford to alienate them by sending 'unsuitable' applicants.

The quiet rebel has to recognise that information given to her by such agencies may be incorrect or incomplete. Where it is refused, she must persist. The result can be an inconclusive waiting game, and the best strategy is probably to dispense with such guidance services totally by using the adverts and other sources of job vacancy information.

Since the Sex Discrimination Act it has become illegal to specify in advertisements for most jobs whether a man or woman is preferred, because sex is not a justifiable criterion for selection. It is fascinating to see how advertisements have evolved a code which indicates which sex is required without actually explicitly saying 'No Woman Need Apply'. A survey showed that unisex adverts directed at men mentioned physique, good health, an apprenticeship, the need for over-time, and, often, possession of a driving licence. Unisex ads for women mentioned typing, appearance, dexterity, and previous experience. Another way of targeting an ad is by placing it only in papers or magazines read exclusively by one sex or the other. Job applicants have been sensitised to the hidden messages of ads and it is rare that they make errors and try for jobs designed for the opposite sex.

Assuming that the quiet rebel ignores career guidance and the unwritten voice of the advert and applies; there is the ultimate hurdle of the personnel manager in charge of hiring. Repeatedly, surveys of personnel managers have shown that the majority regard women *a priori* as inferior to men on all qualities considered by them to be important in a worker. Women, they claim, are not as dependable. Women wishing to do men's work are doubly dubious. Even if they are deemed capable of the job, it is thought that they would cause too much disruption in the workplace and fail to gain acceptance from fellow workers.

Studies of women executives working in supervisory jobs,

gained after affirmative action in the US, have shown that a large majority of the people they worked with reacted favourably. Add this to evidence that women are not less dependable in terms of job turnover, nor in terms of amount of time off through illness, nor in terms of leaving on marriage, and not even in terms of the financial importance of their job to them, and the views of personnel managers stand out for what they are: prejudice.

Legislation has not overcome this prejudice. Changing prejudices is a slow business, particularly when they are rewarding and self-confirmatory, as in this case. After all, if women are excluded, there are no exceptions to show the error of the attitude.

This barrier to selection is the first obstacle in the path of the quiet rebel which is not within her own power to overcome. In order to dismantle it, she may need to act in concert with other women to bring about political and legislative change. Some of the strategies for bringing about such change are discussed in Chapter 8. The single most salient thing she can do is make sure her case is heard. Institutionalised sexism, such as that involved in selection procedures, can only survive because women collude in the cover-up. They fail to publicise what happens. Perhaps the quiet rebel is just a little too quiet, one might even say gagged. Talking about it, even only to friends and family, stalls the onset of paranoia.

Family and Friends as Allies and Enemies

The quiet rebel must try to win the support of her family and her closest friends. The role of the family depends greatly upon the age of the woman. Small-scale surveys of young unmarried women in men's work have shown that they receive considerable encouragement from both parents. This is particularly true if the young woman is gaining academic qualifications and a job carrying high status; if her parents are middle class; and if she has no brothers. Of course, the apparent strength of parental support may be distorted by concentrating only on those girls who choose male-dominated occupations. It may be that only girls with parents amenable to that choice make it in the main.

Evidence about the support offered the older, married quiet rebel is scanty. She has obligations to her husband, her parents and parents-in-law, and their tolerance of her pursuit of men's work may wane. Her work may disrupt the domestic routine, challenge the status hierarchy in the home (if, for instance, she is the main breadwinner), and reshape patterns of socialising. It may also mean that she delays having children, or does not wish to have them at all. Failure to fulfil the 'fertility obligation' can represent a great source of pressure.

The pressures are both internal to the woman and emanate from her family and friends. The external pressures are relatively easy to see. As one woman said, 'My mother saw me as an incubator for the grandchild that would make her a grandmother and let her relive the joys of rearing a baby without the responsibilities. When I showed no signs of providing the plaything, she started with subtle hints which built up to accusation of selfishness and threats that I would regret it when it was too late.' This notion that one is working against a deadline is central to the internal pressure which many women feel. Women who delay starting a family because they wish to pursue their career, whether they are married or not, know that the sand-filled hour glass is running out by the second. They know that there will come a point of no return when it will become difficult or impossible for them to have a child. As they get closer to that point, the decision that they may have previously made not to have children becomes a matter for urgent reconsideration. Virtually every ounce of their socialisation tells them that they are wrong to resist the maternal imperative, yet many know that to comply will be a serious setback in their working life. So often the quiet rebel finds herself in her mid-thirties stranded between her career ambitions and her desire to mother. That she should have to make such an invidious choice is clearly a product of the historical position of women in the family and labour market. But it is interesting how many highly successful quiet rebels see the imposition of the choice as inevitable and in some senses just. One of the few women directors of a social services department in Britain commented, when asked 'It is difficult for women to choose between a career and a family commitment. Having made the choice to have a family, it is then difficult to get back into the profession at senior management level. Very few women apply for jobs at deputy level, never mind director level. This is the chief problem, rather than any form of prejudice or discrimination against women.' She did not consider having to make the choice itself a form of discrimination. She had chosen career rather than family, and presumably considers it the fault of other women that they have not done the same in order to gain advancement.

If the quiet rebel has children, the problems may be compounded. Continuing at work may be extremely difficult, since she must then become dependent on others caring for the children. There have been many studies of the stress of continuing occupational and parental roles; they both confirm and disprove many myths. It is hazardous to make general-isations about the costs and benefits of employment to mothers of young children, since they vary with the specific circum-stances: the number of children she has, her attitude to work, and the number of hours worked, not to mention the type of job. Most of the studies calculate the impact of work by comparing working with non-working mothers. This entails two problems. Firstly, the two groups are rarely identical in every respect other than employment, so it is impossible to say whether work or other background factors produce any measured differences. Secondly, it is quite difficult to measure stress and conflict effectively. So the generalisations have to be treated with caution.

The majority of studies show employed mothers are generally happier, have greater self-esteem, feel competent, and believe they have social standing. There are no marked differences in mental health, though the employed seem less prone to depression. Most working mothers experience 'role conflict'. This means they feel their two roles are contradictory, and this prevents either being performed satisfactorily. The result is a heightened sense of guilt about being at work. One relatively young mother indicates the change of attitudes motherhood may bring: 'I was anxious not to take too much maternity leave, since my job was fixed term. My daughter was born at the beginning of February and I returned to full-time work in mid-April. However, I was miserable, largely because of seeing so little of my daughter. I went part-time but decided then to resign, as I felt very strongly I wanted to bring up my baby myself.' Role conflict of this sort recedes in the middle class, where women hold less tenaciously to the 'good mother' self-image. But largely women cope with role conflict not by seeking to change the obligations attached to each role but by spreading themselves ever more thinly in an attempt to fulfil each perfectly. This is exemplified in a study which looked at the number of hours in a week women engaged in high status professional jobs spent in professional and domestic work. Single childless women spent 58 hours at professional work and 23 hours in domestic work; the figures for single women with one or more children were 57 hours and 33 hours; for married women without children they were 61 hours and 18 hours; and for married women with children 48 hours and 60 hours respectively. This means that married women with children worked 108 hours a week. Given that there are only 168 hours in the week and that even the quiet rebel has to sleep, say, 56 hours, these women had on average 4 hours each week not working. That is what might be called taking oneself to the limit. Yet, when asked whether they felt overworked, none of the women, all of whom were working hours in excess of those required by two full-time jobs, claimed that they were particularly overworked. They felt that they only worked as much as other women in their position, so could make no claim to special hardship.

Studies of women in the professions who have had children and who had a career break to rear them point to the fact that many would not make that choice in retrospect. One older woman engineer stated: 'If, in the 1980s, I had recently married, I would seriously consider delaying having a family until I could afford domestic help and then I would keep my job.' Another said: 'Were I at the beginning of the cycle now, I suspect I would try to work continuously, but this would have been quite impossible in the climate of eighteen years ago and given the salaries paid to young engineers.' She went on to say that as a consequence of her break, she was earning only half the salary she could have expected to be getting if she had continued. These older women, who felt that they had made a mistake in leaving their work for their children, were not just complaining about lack of advancement and low salaries. They were also stressing that they were being 'wasted'. Their skills, knowledge and energy were being allowed to moulder and become redundant. During their break they had no way of offering anything to their professions or of keeping abreast of developments in them. Yet all could see ways in which this might be done through flexible employment arrangements and courses to 'top up' knowledge.

The impact of a working mother upon her children has long been a matter of debate. The consensus now seems to be that the continual presence of the mother is unnecessary even for young infants. As long as the alternative caretakers are relatively constant and of high quality, they do not negatively affect infant development or the relationship between the mother and her child. As the child gets older, the employment of the mother can have positive psychological benefits. Working mothers have more autonomous and independent teenagers, their daughters are likely to have greater self-esteem, and they are likely to have higher levels of aspirations, be high achievers, and move into non-traditional occupations. The implication is that the guilt women feel about work is ill-founded, though it may be this that drives them to offer their children more than they would otherwise get.

This discussion has centred more on what mothers working in any job feel and do, rather than just on the quiet rebel, but it is the essential backdrop to her activities. In dealing with her family, the quiet rebel whether married or single needs two sets of skills: organisational skills and negotiation skills. The sheer number of hours she works means that she has to organise to survive, not only herself but everybody else too. Everyone can learn to be a good organiser. It requires practice and patience. The keys to success are anticipation and planning. Anticipate and specify the goal (the target, objective, desired end), delineate the steps necessary to achieve it (simply and in sequence), and, most important, outline possible hitches and include contingency plans (alternative ways round). Most working women live by the Holy Writ of the List. The List says what has to be done, when, by whom and, often, how much it will cost. But nine-tenths of organisation is routine and ritual. Instituting routines means that you can go on to autopilot: you do not have to think and plan because it is always done this way. It is strange how rapid routinisation can be. Many women report how stressful it is when they first return to work after child-rearing and how within months the pattern becomes calm and manageable. Essentially, what happens is that they erect a routine around the work: one which involves them in longer hours and requires more stamina, but to which they rapidly adjust.

Negotiation skills are more difficult to acquire; many of them are considered in detail later on but a number of points are particularly important with regard to the family. At the heart of negotiation is the ability to see clearly both one's own interests and those of the people with whom one deals. Faulty perception of the other person's desires and motives is at the heart of much conflict. The quiet rebel needs to be particularly sensitive to how her family reacts to her work and the changes it brings. She has to make sure she knows how the individual members feel. This does not mean that she should allow it to override her own feelings, but it is only by accurately understanding theirs that she can act in a manner which will gain their confidence and support.

Negotiation revolves around the manipulation of facts and rewards. Acting in such a manipulative way in your own home may be repugnant to you. The cynic would say it is for everyone's good in the end: chronic conflict helps no one; unilateral capitulation will not help you; and compromise requires negotiation.

The quiet rebel has to wean her family off the image of her solely as a dutiful daughter, succouring mother, and conventional worker. She is engaging in a process of persuasion. The single most important factor in determining whether an attempt at persuasion is successful is persistence. The quiet rebel has to be persistent and, secondly, consistent in the message she transmits to her family. She has to tell them her work does not change her feelings for them, that she is determined to succeed at it, and that they will also benefit from it in the long run. Every quiet rebel will have unique family problems to deal with, and the messages she gives will depend upon what they are. Regardless of the content of the message, it must be consistent, unwavering, and persistently delivered. The watchwords are: know your family and be consistent and persistent in what you tell them.

A quiet rebel must choose friends carefully and normally does. Young unmarried women moving into men's work tend to abandon friends and boyfriends who fail to be supportive.

Jenny, aged twenty-four, a second mate on a ship in the merchant marine, expresses attitudes which are typical of the younger single quiet rebel in the 1980s: 'I cannot afford to be making excuses for myself and my job to friends or boyfriends. The men on board ship have accepted me now, although whenever I move to a new one, the old battles are refought, but ashore men often find my work a joke. You know, the whole battery of sick jokes about tattoos and mermaids. I don't try to persuade them. They are not worth the time and effort. I am only interested in people who can accept me for what I am. The men I go out with have to understand that I'm not interested in the kitchen sink and I may be off on a run to Brazil tomorrow with no regrets.' Older women in such jobs tend to have fewer friends, not surprisingly, since they have so little time to socialise outside of work. The friendships normally engendered at work may be denied the quiet rebel, because she flaunts many of the workplace conventions by merely being there and doing her job. Isolation is a common experience for the quiet rebel. Yet this may be potentially less damaging than inappropriate friendships.

Friends are reference points. One checks one's attitudes and values against those of friends to make sure they are correct and acceptable. Friends are sounding boards for new ideas; a safe audience for one's secret dreams. Friends are depositories for self-revelation and self-doubt. Friends are a generalised yardstick for self-appraisal and insight. For all these reasons, choosing the wrong friends can be disastrous.

The quiet rebel needs friends who have similar values with regard to the family and work. If they do not, they have to offer sustenance in other ways, maybe practical help with childcare or perhaps by reminding her of the roots of her earlier life. Friends who provide neither similarity nor complementarity are costly investments. They can generate disquieting comparisons. For instance, the quiet rebel who has time to clean and garden adequately but not to perfection, would do well to avoid making comparisons with a green-fingered, houseproud friend. Dissatisfaction with oneself is the only product of such comparisons, yet they are inevitable if the friendship is close. Some women maintain such friendships by an imaginative discounting procedure which automatically cuts in when they walk into the spotless house of a friend to whisper excuses for their own chaotic untidiness. They justify their own failures in comparison with the friend and retain the friendship. As a temporary measure this may work, but, in the long term, continual self-justification is no basis for a friendship.

The quiet rebel needs the support of family and friends and has to use skills of organisation and negotiation to achieve it, besides being willing to amputate obsolescent relationships. Beyond that, of course, when the proverbial chips are down, she has to be able to stand alone and feel proud that she can.

Remediable Obstacles to Breaking In

This chapter has painted a black picture of the barriers facing the woman choosing to become a quiet rebel. There is the stereotyping of womanhood and the sex role prescriptions; there are childhood conceptions of work; there is the negligence of the education system and the biases in the selection procedures; and there is the complex dynamic of family and friends. Reviewing the barriers, it is necessary to remember that despite them every year more women do join the ranks of the quiet rebels. The barriers are not insurmountable. This chapter has offered only a few grappling hooks; there are more to come.

Further Reading

Glennon, L. M., *Women and Dualism: A Sociology of Knowledge Analysis.*

New York: Longman, 1979.

Chetwynd, J. and Hartnett, O. (eds), *The Sex Role System: Psychological and Sociological Perspectives*. London: Routledge and Kegan Paul, 1978.

Archer, J. and Lloyd, B., *Sex and Gender*. Harmondsworth: Penguin, 1982.

Lipshitz, S. (ed.), *Tearing the Veil*. London: Routledge and Kegan Paul, 1978.

Deem, R. (ed.), *Schooling for Women's Work*. London: Routledge and Kegan Paul, 1980.

Weitzman, L., *Sex Role Socialization*. Palo Alto: Mayfield, 1979.

Oakley, A., *Subject Women*. Glasgow: Fontana, 1981.

Yogev, S., 'Are professional women overworked? Objective versus subjective perception of role loads.' *Journal of Occupational Psychology*, 55, 165–69, 1982.

Lewis, S. and Cooper, C. L., 'The stress of combining occupational and parental roles: a review of the literature.' *Bulletin of the British Psychological Society*, 36, 341–45, 1983.

Gilligan, C., *In a Different Voice*. Cambridge, Mass.: Harvard, 1982.

Sayer, J., *Sexual Contradictions*. London: UPP, 1985.

Weitz, S., *Sex Roles*. New York: Oxford, 1977.

Weitzman, L.J., *Sex Role Socialization*. Palo Alto, Cal.: Mayfield, 1979.

Chapter Three
FEAR OF FAILURE, FEAR OF SUCCESS

Above all, the quiet rebel has to believe in herself. She requires constancy of purpose and an overwhelming desire to succeed despite all the barriers. One idea has to be tattooed across her psyche: that *she is capable of success and wants success*. Therein lies the crux of a serious psychological barrier, for a number of factors conspire to make her doubt her capacity and need for success. Some of these stem from early childhood, others from the way she will be treated at work. They have to be overcome, and the quiet rebel has to learn how to cope realistically with both failure and success.

Failing Blame and Discounting Success

Over the last decade, psychologists have studied how people explain their own and others' successes and failures. This has been part of a major enterprise to discover how people explain behaviour and events generally. Understanding how people explain what happens to them and around them is important, because the explanation may dictate how they react. For instance, if a child breaks a valuable piece of china, her mother's reaction will depend on the explanation given for the breakage. If the child did it accidentally, punishment might be considered inappropriate; whereas, if it was deliberate, punishment to fit the crime might be devised. The child's fate depends on how her mother chooses to explain what has happened. The development of a theory which can predict what explanation will be given is therefore valuable. The theory concerned has been labelled 'attribution theory' because it is about how people attribute causes to occurrences.

Attribution theorists have argued that, in the main, people are rational in forming explanations; they use information logically to draw conclusions about the causes or reasons for what happens. However, people are not computers, and their calculations are subject to bias which is not random but consistent and patterned. So, for instance, people have a tendency when explaining their own behaviour to attribute it to the circumstances in which it occurs. You get drunk at a party and you claim it was because you were in the middle of a family row. In direct contrast, people explain the behaviour of others in terms of their character or personality. Watching you get drunk, other people will claim it is because you are an inveterate old soak, and depressive to boot.

For our present purposes, the biases which are interesting concern attributions for success and failure. One striking finding that recurs across the Western world is that there is a consistent sex difference in attributions for success and failure. If they fail, women attribute it to their personal inadequacies: they did not try hard enough, were too stupid, or were lacking skill. Men who fail blame anything but themselves: they had bad luck, someone did the dirty on them, the task was unfair. On the other hand, women will not take the 'blame' for their own success, and this is particularly acute where the success involves pursuits normally regarded as a male prerogative. Success, women put down to chance, someone's error, someone's kindness, the unusual simplicity of the job, or the strange weakness of the opposition. Where women fear to tread, men rush in. Men are willing to accept responsibility for their own successes, acknowledging them to be the product of their own talents. Amazingly, this sex difference has been found in children as young as four years of age.

Of course, these studies describe the average male and average female responses to success and failure. Individual women may stand against the trend, and the quiet rebel certainly needs to do so. She has to avoid the trap of these conventional ways of responding, since both wallowing in self-blame for failure and discounting success are non-adaptive. Both offer less than an accurate view of reality and consequently prevent appropriate action. In order to evolve effective strategies for coping with these habits, it is necessary first to consider why they may have developed.

Success is Unsexing

Women do not, in general, like to be considered successful. Minor or transient successes, in activities recognised to fall strictly within the female domain, are permissible. More than that, especially if achieved in pursuits unusual for a woman, such as those central to the existence of the quiet rebel, is shunned. Women are taught from childhood that they should not excel; proficiency is sufficient. Any manifestation of excellence, they are told, will make them conspicuous, unlike other women and, most importantly, unattractive. The successful woman, simply because she is successful, is deemed less of a woman.

Children learn this code early. Studies have shown that children as young as five years old will describe a successful person as more happy, calm, fearless and wise than someone who fails, but a women who succeeds is considered less honest, attractive, nice and more selfish than her male counterparts.

Adults elaborate on this process which demeans the successful woman. A woman's successes are much more likely to be attributed to temporary factors having nothing to do with the woman herself. Outsiders emulate the woman's own tendency to discount her success. This is particularly strange since one of the strongest attribution biases, as mentioned earlier, is the trend for observers to explain another person's behaviour in terms of personal characteristics. Not only do observers claim a woman's success is not due to her own qualities, but they also argue that her success will be short-lived. They predict her luck will run out and she will return to her 'proper place'. Even this presumption is topped by the strong tendency that observers have to refuse to accept that the woman is successful in the first place. A series of studies have shown that people given evidence that a woman has succeeded in some task will challenge the facts more readily than they do when told a man has succeeded. If they are ultimately made to acknowledge the facts, they set up more stringent criteria for a woman to fulfil before they will validate her success. They are just plainly unwilling to allow that a woman has succeeded.

These findings conjure up a cautionary picture: a woman has to do more in the first place to be awarded success; if she gets it, she will not be credited with having brought it about; and, once successful, she will be assumed to possess various unpleasant personal characteristics. All of which serves to emphasise that success and womanhood are felt to be orthogonal axes. As Margaret Mead put it in 1950, 'success is unsexing'. To choose success, is to lose some essential ingredient of femininity.

It could be argued then that only a fool fails to fear success, since it carries so many aversive connotations. It could equally well be argued that only a greater fool fails to conquer that fear, since success carries so many advantages. Perhaps, women fear success more because for them the disadvantages are more numerous and strike more directly at the heart of their identity.

The evidence of fear of success may explain why women seek to discount their success when asked to describe its causes. By

shifting the responsibility for their success to outside themselves, women deflect claims that they are not 'proper women'.
You cannot be blamed for success which is thrust upon you by
circumstances against your wishes. Just like a foetus, a success
can be aborted; flushed out in this case by an unrealistic
attribution.

For the quiet rebel, discounting success and accepting
responsibility for failure is especially damaging. Successes are
not so frequent that they can be squandered. They are required
to bolster any flagging in the ego of a woman who is daily
standing outside the mainstream. Make the most of successes.
The quiet rebel who withstands so many attacks on her identity
as a woman has to accustom herself to the threat posed by
success. If she does not, then her other struggles are deprived of
meaning. There is no point in battling to gain men's work
unless you also seek to succeed in it. The quiet rebel who fails
knocks one more nail in the coffin of any other woman following
in her footsteps. It is hardly surprising then that it is argued
that women fear success, but the fear of success is by no means
an exclusive property of women. Success carries its own
penalties; success demands even greater success. People talk
about getting on a treadmill that goes faster and faster until
they cannot keep upright. Some people respond well to
increased pressure; others crack and refuse to run like a
hamster in a cage. Opting out in this way can be conscious or
beneath awareness. Drop out and burn out are two responses
common in this situation. Instead of trying to gain success,
some people drop out: they no longer compete, and they may
evolve complex rationalisations to justify their abdication, like
that the system's values stink. Other people carry on trying
but burn out. This is most frequent in the 'people professions'
(medicine, teaching, social work, etc.), where the carers are
drained dry by continuous demands for emotional and physical
support from others. People who were kind, sensitive and
empathic become callous, cynical and selfish. But burn out can

occur just as easily in the business world, where energy, drive, enthusiasm, new ideas and so on are continually demanded if success is to follow success. Its signs are manifest: people start to withdraw into their shell a little more everyday; they do not make suggestions and fail to respond to them; effectively, they do just enough to make their job tick over and no more. Burn out signifies a withdrawal from the race for success.

Attributing failure to personal inadequacies, when failures are not infrequent, is a recipe for desperation. It becomes important to the quiet rebel when looking for a job. She is likely to receive many rejections, and she is most likely to take this as a slight on her talent, skills or experience. This response is likely to lead to despondency and ultimately to withdrawal from the job market. Instead, the quiet rebel has to examine how far her rejection is a result of the idiocy of employers, the vagaries of the market, or worldwide economic trends. The woman who knows that these factors account for her failures will carry on applying for jobs; the impact upon her self-confidence and self-esteem will not be anywhere near as rapid or as deep. Persistence in the labour market is nine-tenths of the battle, even in times of high unemployment. Women who fail to persist, fail full stop. The message is clear: try to evaluate sensibly how far you are personally responsible for failure and do not give up too soon.

Self-Handicapping

While people may not wish to succeed, they will very rarely admit that blunt truth to themselves. After all, society places extraordinary emphasis upon success. Competition is the name of the game and everyone is expected to play — even women, though they are simply not expected to win. Little girls are told: 'You must try' and, in an undertone, 'but it does not matter if you do not quite do it.' So the young woman receives a beautifully ambivalent message: she should try to succeed but she should not succeed, because success is so unfeminine. This is a classic *double bind* situation which demands two mutually exclusive things of a person, so that whatever she does, she does wrong.

Various strategies are employed in dealing with this double bind; one entails *self-handicapping*. People using self-handicapping take part in the struggle which is expected of them but they make sure that they are hampered in some way that means that they fail. This serves two functions: they avoid success, but they also have an excuse for their failure which makes it more socially acceptable. For instance, researchers have found that professional sportsmen and women engage in self-handicapping sometimes before big matches: they fail to turn up to practice sessions, or do not fully involve themselves in training programmes, or 'accidentally' strain a muscle just before the match. Self-handicapping of this sort produces ready-made, viable excuses and allows them to duck the trauma of success.

Of course, often people do not realise consciously that they are engaging in self-handicapping. The salesperson who gets paralytic drunk the night before a big deal is not usually deliberately sabotaging her ability to concentrate or make a good impression. The women facing a job interview who knows that she should appear serious and competent does not commit the premeditated murder of her hopes by giggling or wearing a flamboyant and totally inappropriate costume. Self-handicapping can be quite unintentional because it can become habitual. Some people do it in at least one aspect of their lives, but if they are lucky, it is in an area which is not fundamental to their health and happiness.

Helen, an academic in her mid-forties, typifies the self-handicapping syndrome. On the surface she wants promotion; she has been a university lecturer for twenty years and should be moving up the management hierarchy. She knows that to do this she has to show a high level of commitment to her department, and that this is measured in terms of ability to bring research grants into it, in terms of involvement in departmental social life, and in the level of administrative duties and student contact accepted. She works hard at her research and is productive in publications. She has good relations with students and is recognised as a good teacher. All she basically needs to do is participate effectively in the social life of her department, make a big self-glorifying noise, blow her own trumpet, and she can expect a promotion. However, she consistently fails to do this. She fails to go to parties she knows will be boring. She only speaks at meetings when she has something to say — unlike many of her male colleagues. She is no expert at self-praise: her boastfulness is woefully small. Her persistence in this relatively low-profile behaviour ensures her promotion will be withheld. She is not playing the game by the rules. She is self-handicapping, not, perhaps, consciously, but she is doing it nevertheless. She knows the rules of the game but cannot bring herself to play by them.

She is unlikely to get promotion, and when it does not come she can say, indeed she already does say, 'It is not because my work is no good, it is because my play is no good.' Failure against such a standard may be easier to bear than failure in terms of the value of research or publications. The self-handicapping not only ensures failure, it excuses it.

The pressure on the quiet rebel to succumb to self-handicapping is ferocious. She will have learnt in a general way, as every woman does, that success is bad for her and that she is, in any case, unlikely to attain it. What easier way to salve her pride than by self-handicapping? The temptation is undoubtedly great, but the penalties for capitulation even greater. She will trap herself in failure; enmesh herself in a web of faded dreams and forlorn hopes. Above all she must not self-handicap; after all, other people are busily heaping handicaps upon her all the time.

The quiet rebel has to be alert to the signals for the onset of self-handicapping. It starts with doubting your own abilities to succeed. The next phase entails casting around for reasons why one might legitimately fail; reasons that will not reflect too badly upon oneself. The final phase requires manipulation so that you find yourself a victim of those legitimate reasons for failure. The rot has to be stopped in the second phase. Everyone has self-doubts, and these can be highly adaptive, making you work harder to bring about your own development and growth. The trick lies in directing self-doubt into activities which are productive rather than destructive in the longer term. Self-handicapping may be a transient answer, but it warps the user over time. So, as soon as you find yourself looking for a justification for failure, you have to recognise the pit that lies before your feet ready to snap you up. Vigilance is the watchword.

One form of self-handicapping to which the quiet rebel is particularly subject deserves special mention. This is the tendency to inflate the problems lying in her path to success. To some extent this is understandable, since they are many and vicious. However, their exaggeration to the point where they become totally unhandleable horrors is self-handicapping. The woman who blows up problems out of all proportion is justifying her anticipated failure but, equally, making it infinitely more likely. Scaring herself, she withdraws from the battle prematurely or will not devote all her resources to it.

The quiet rebel has to relegate horror stories to the late-night movie. She has to analyse problems realistically, place them in context, and respond unemotionally. This may mean taking extra time to collect information and the restraint of spontaneity. If it means evading the punishments for self-handicapping, it will be worthwhile.

The Importance of Locus of Control

People differ in how far they feel in control of themselves and of what happens to them. Some people feel that they are self-determining: they are in control. Others feel they are at the whim of events and the will of everyone else. The former have been said to have internal locus of control, the latter external locus of control. Naturally, these are the extreme poles of a continuum. The majority fall in the middle of the range, and feel in control or controlled according to circumstances. Those at the extremes, however, have an habitual way of seeing the world and what happens to them which is erroneous. It is inaccurate because it fails to take account of the facts or, rather, the facts are distorted to pander to the preconception.

Neither internal nor external locus of control is desirable. Internal locus of control has been implicated in the genesis of depression. Depressives tend to have internal locus of control, perceive the world as stable and any problem encountered as global. Faced with an unpleasant event, the potential depressive sees herself as responsible for bringing it about, believes it will continue a long time, and that it will affect all aspects of her life. The conglomeration of these three factors can drive her over the edge into depression. Meanwhile external locus of control can be equally damaging. It engenders feelings of helplessness, a lowering of self-esteem, and the elimination of any sense of competence or autonomy.

The origins of these two styles of thinking (they are often referred to as cognitive styles) seem to lie in patterns of learning in early childhood. They grow out of the way children's actions are regarded or punished by those who care for them. Internal locus of control is developed where the child's rewards and punishments are contingent upon her actions. So, for instance, the child who misbehaves and is punished immediately or, if she is punished later, has it explained to her that it fits her crime, develops a sense of internal control. She feels that she determines her own fate. She finds that rewards follow compliance, as the sun trails the moon, regularly. She knows she is in control because her actions are tied systematically to their own outcomes; she can predict what will happen as a consequence. The child will not have set up the rules of the reward and punishment game, but she knows them and plays by them to her own advantage. External locus of control originates in the unpredictability of rewards and punishments. In some families, a child will receive reward and punishment virtually randomly; they are not fixed to her behaviour. Sometimes she is punished for doing wrong, sometimes it is ignored, sometimes she is even rewarded. The child never knows what to expect and can make no predictions of the outcomes of her actions. She learns rapidly that it is not within her power to control what happens to her and assumes an external locus of control.

Basically, people who feel that they are in control of their lives and do not believe in the powerlessness of the individual in the face of fate have an internal locus of control. People with an external locus of control believe their destiny is charted in the stars, or a product of chance, or manipulated by others with power; whichever it is, they know that they are not-self-determining. Of course, only a minority of people have a totally internal or totally external locus of control. Most people hold to a mixture of the two. Nevertheless, people do exist who reside at either extreme.

Later experiences, outside the confines of the family, may fail to impinge upon the cognitive style developed in childhood. By that stage, the perception of events is distorted and facts are not countenanced if they disturb existing predelictions. They may also be perpetuated because no one chooses to point out to the person that these non-adaptive biases exist.

Self-observation will reveal the existence of biases. The quiet rebel needs to be realistic in calculating when she has control and when she is subject to circumstances beyond her control. She needs to monitor whether she has a persistent tendency to assume she is determining what happens or to perceive herself as externally controlled. If she does notice a bias, she needs to quell it. One way to do this is to pay attention to a broader range of information pertinent to the situation, so that she comes to see what happens from a number of different perspectives. She should make a habit of trying to evolve a number of alternative explanations for what happens and then test out their validity against all the relevant evidence. Another tactic involves comparing one's own perceptions with those of other people. Having concluded, in line perhaps with one's normal internal locus of control, that one has things under control, ask someone else how they see it. When others contradict your own version of reality, it should be taken seriously and certainly not dismissed. They may not, by any means, be correct all the time, but even their errors may instruct you in new aspects of the situation. The main message is: rely on realism not reflex. Use all the information sources at your command to judge rationally where control lies. Remember that it is not lodged irrevocably in one place, whether inside or outside yourself. The situation interacts with your own powers to determine afresh the locus of control in each specific instance. In truth, control is never either totally internal or external—these are tidy myths of a childish mind.

Learning to be Helpless

There is some evidence to suggest that women are more likely to fall at the external end of the locus of control continuum than the internal pole. Women are more likely to see themselves as victims of circumstance rather than mistresses of their own fate. This is, of course, compatible with everything that has been said about their responses to success and the societal pressures that push them to reject self-determination. These processes are accompanied by a further phenomenon known as *learned helplessness*.

Learned helplessness is exactly what it appears. The phrase

is used to describe what happens when people who are reasonably capable of organising their own lives are prevented from doing so; when things are done for them, people learn to be incapable of doing them for themselves. The process was mapped in homes for the elderly. Old people would arrive quite lively, having looked after themselves for a lifetime before entering the home. They would be subjected to a régime which proceeded to deskill them by giving them no opportunity to make decisions for themselves and ensuring that they did not need to use whatever skills they had. When things are done for you, you soon lose the knack of doing them for yourself. You learn helplessness.

The disabled report similar experiences. Cripples describe how people try their utmost to offer assistance, to the point of actually being offended if help proves unnecessary. The cripple who can cope is inundated with redundant help, and it is the easy option to forget to try to cope. Helplessness can be a career.

It seems that often people are actually rewarded for showing helplessness. There are all sorts of reasons why this should be so. For everyone who is helpless, there is someone who is helpful. Helpfulness is addictive: a good deed a day keeps much guilt away. The helpless person who shows signs of rejecting help is actually removing the gratification. If they try, they are shown that it is not appropriate. Mute acceptance of help offered, meanwhile, is encouraged and fostered. In institutional settings the reason for rewarding helplessness may be more prosaic. Passive inmates are easier to handle, and can be shaped to the requirements of the bureaucracy rather than vice versa.

Learned helplessness, even that in senile patients, can be reversed with careful rehabilitation, as long as the will of the patient can be harnessed. People have to want to regain control, to rediscover their skills and recover the ability to make decisions.

Learned helplessness may seem a long cry from the quiet rebel, yet it may be important. Many highly successful women, who have broken the traditions regarding sex roles and survived, talk about their hidden fear of independence. Collette Dowling has called it 'the Cinderella complex'. Even at the summit of self-determination, these women crave dependence. Instead of being autonomous and responsible for their own lives, they would like a wonderful Prince Charming, doubtless on a snowy white (highly phallic) charger, to come dashing up to sweep them away from all care and all decisions. They want to be able to relinquish control and feel safe in the strong hands of someone else.

A barrister in her early fifties with two children, a husband and a reputation as a fearsome opponent, describes how she copes with her own sneaky yearning for dependence. 'Once I finish work for the day, especially after a really heated courtroom debate, I like to fold up my intellect and shelve it. I like to become totally indecisive, I like things to be imposed upon me. I shed all responsibility like a snake casts its skin.' She is temporarily portraying the helpless female. In her case, of course, it is very definitely only temporary. She uses helplessness as a time for recharging her drive to control and dominate. Not many women employ their Cinderella complex so productively.

It seems supremely ironic that women who have fought, sometimes literally, tooth and nail to achieve independence, not just financially but from the throes of sex role stereotypy, want to throw it back. It is instructive that the form their dream of dependence takes reflects a residue of childhood notions of the ideal male-female relationship. In it, he is heroic, dependable, rich and handsome; she is transformed from rags to riches, urchin to princess, by his love. In specifying that she rather fancies this perfect arrangement if she is to lose her independence, the quiet rebel may merely be signalling that she has no intention of losing it. It is not a real possibility. The man does not exist who could live up to that story line. These women are telling themselves a fairy tale. One can imagine them saying, 'One day my prince will come but, in the meantime, I'll settle for being Lord Mayor of London myself.'

Indeed, some women find that the fairy-tale ideal cankers their view of real men. Quiet rebels who are single often report that they are searching for the man who will make them wish to act out the stereotypical female role. They remain single and a rebel only because they cannot find the man who would make helplessness acceptable. Jean, at thirty-five is rich and powerful, managing her own small but profitable fabric design and dye firm; she is unmarried but wants to be a wife. She has no illusions, however: 'I want to marry someone who will allow me to stop working, who will be more capable in business than I and who will offer me romance. I do not expect to find him, but I will not settle for anything less, so I shall go on ensuring my own financial future and snatch any romance which is passing.' Such women are seeking voluntary helplessness on their own conditions. There is a world of difference between voluntary and compulsory helplessness.

For women who have not achieved independence, learned helplessness may be a more serious problem and compulsory. It can operate in a selective manner, applying to only a narrow band of skills. For instance, many women claim not to be able to deal with money matters effectively. They claim that they cannot keep track of money; that they will spend indiscriminately; or that they simply find the intricacies of banking and saving beyond them. All these claims can be symptoms of one branch of learned helplessness. Women who say these things have often been deprived of control of their own finances by male relatives and, over time, have come to accept it as inevitable due to their helplessness.

The feeling is often accompanied by statements like: 'What's the point of trying to understand how to balance the books? My father always used to say I had no head for figures'; 'I don't try to understand what happened to the money, it's always eluded my grasp ever since I was a child. My brother used to keep my pocket money and buy me things I wanted, he never seemed to run over budget'; or, 'No one let me have any dealings with money when I was younger, and it seemed natural to leave everything to my husband. Now I'm divorced, I get into all sorts of difficulties'. These quotes come from women who, in other areas of their lives, are quite self-sufficient. They have clearly learnt that in money matters they were not supposed or expected to have control.

Overcoming these beliefs about one's helplessness is no simple matter. In tackling them, counselling may be required. Certainly, you need to get support from others who will be able to teach you the skills you lack. The main thing is to realise that skill deficits can be retrieved. New skills can be learnt. The quiet rebel who feels helpless in a particular area should ask herself two questions: (i) In what ways am I rewarded for being unable to do this? and (ii), What skills do I lack and where can I acquire them? In answering the first question one sometimes finds the rewards outweigh the costs of helplessness and progress to the second question may be unnecessary. Even if this is so, the exercise in self-exploration can be valuable because it highlights what are probably covert motives and needs. The quiet rebel, like anyone else, needs a lucid understanding of her own motives and needs if she is to avoid inner conflict and frustration of her goals.

Fighting the Internal Obstacles

This chapter has focused on a network of psychological hurdles that the quiet rebel must expect to face. She must avoid finding inappropriate explanations for her own success and failure. She must counter any fear she has of success. She must not succumb to the temptation to self-handicap. She must calculate realistically the locus of control for her actions. She must strictly limit any tendency to learned helplessness. These five commandments may not be written on tablets of stone, but they should be inscribed on the quiet rebel's heart. Honouring them is dependent upon self-awareness and realism. She needs to be vigilant against the worst excesses of her own secret motives, needs and habits. In addition, she needs to be responsive to all possible sources of information, so that she can come to rational conclusions about the reasons for actions and events. In this way, she becomes immune to both horror stories and fairy tales, and comes to know through experience that success is good for you.

Further Reading

Hawkins, R. P. and Pingree, S., 'A developmental exploration of the fear of success phenomenon as cultural stereotype.' *Sex Roles, 4 (4)*, 539–47, 1978.

Dowling, C., *The Cinderella Complex: Women's Hidden Fear of Independence*. Glasgow: Fontana, 1982.

Horner, M. S., 'Toward an understanding of the achievement-related conflicts in women.' *Journal of Social Issues, 28 (2)*, 157–76, 1972.

Weiner, B. (ed.), *Achievement motivation and attribution theory*. Morristown, N. J.: General Learning Press, 1974.

Jones, E. E., Kanouse, D. E., Kelley, H. H., Nisbett, R. E., Valnis, S. and Weiner, B., *Attribution: Perceiving the causes of behaviour*. Morristown, N. J.: General Learning Press, 1972.

Jones, E. E., and Berglas, S., 'Control of attributions about the self through self-handicapping strategies: the appeal of alcohol and the role of underachievement.' *Personality and Social Psychology Bulletin, 4*, 200–206, 1978.

Rotter, J. B. 'Generalised expectancies for internal versus external control of reinforcement.' *Psychological Monographs, 80*, 1, 1966.

Seligman, M. E. P., *Helplessness: On Depression, Development and Death*. San Francisco: W. H. Freeman, 1975.

Chapter Four

RELATIONSHIPS AT WORK

This chapter is concerned with the relationships which develop at work with men and with other women. The central argument is that these relationships are patterned, and that the same type of pattern recurs across quite different work contexts. The relationships with which the quiet rebel has to cope have the same essential ingredients whether she doctors trees or people, drives a tube train or a dumper truck, captains commerce or an oil tanker. The way the relationship is dressed may vary considerably, the language used may differ, the material props may be substituted, and the currency of reward or punishment may fluctuate. But these are mere outward, and transient, manifestations of the true nature of a relationship. The pattern underneath lies untouched; a template for the growth of friendship and enmity across job and time. Some slight modification to the patterns may be introduced by the unique combination of age, status and personality of the individual quiet rebel; but in important aspects the template wields its invidious sway. Only by making a conscious decision to shatter the mould can the quiet rebel establish custom-built relationships.

Ready-Made Relationships

The prefabricated pattern of relationships that the quiet rebel
is expected to step into in the workplace is a product of quite a
complex set of dynamics. The arrival of the quiet rebel on the
scene threatens the existing system of relationships. She
occupies a position normally filled by a man, but she will rarely
be expected to act like a man. The preconceptions and
assumptions about the person who would normally do her job
are deemed inapplicable; whether they really are, of course, is
questionable. Inevitably, the quiet rebel necessitates change on
the part of her co-workers. The men may well find themselves,
for the first time, in direct competition with or subordinate to a
woman. One young man, a post-doctorate chemist, typifies the
problem: 'After finishing my PhD I joined a research team
which was headed by a young woman not much older than I. I
had never had a woman dictating what I should do before. I did
not doubt her ability, but found it difficult to accept her
decisions without arguing. I wanted to emphasise my own
ability in a way that I found unnecessary with male superiors. I
found it positively galling to be told what to do by her in front of
other women research staff. It was quite a shock to me
recognising how I felt, because I reckoned that I was really
egalitarian.' The women may find themselves supervised by or
provided with technical services by another woman. One
young manager reports how she found herself embarrassed by
having her own secretary: 'I could not adjust to the idea that
she expected me to be telling her what to do. She was too much
like my mother to feel happy with ordering her about. I ended
up by trying to please her which she found confusing and I
found frustrating.' The sexual division of power is shifted.

Modifications in the balance of power can threaten all
concerned. The men no longer have exclusive control of a
preserve of economic activity. They may find themselves
querying whether this means that their identification with the

job offers less cache. The entry of women into an occupation has been known to lower its status, and the men may see their status start to crumble before their very eyes. They can certainly no longer use the job as a unique symbol of masculinity; work done by a woman fast loses its machismo image. The women, in their turn, can no longer feel the security of subservience. They can no longer be sure that they are immune from such work. They can no longer make blasé excuses for not having done it themselves. Most of all, they can no longer relate to the occupant of that job as a woman to a man. In the disruption, envy may flow from both men and women. Fear is even more probable. Any change is fearful; one which rocks the dominance hierarchy can induce terror, not to mention hatred.

The way envy, fear and hatred get translated into relationship patterns with the quiet rebel depends on how those concerned normally deal with such emotions. Most commonly, the quiet rebel is de-individualised. De-individualisation entails treating someone as a member of a category of people rather than as a unique individual with a special set of characteristics, emotions and skills. Co-workers reduce the attention they pay to the real facts about the quiet rebel; they are not interested in her as a real person. She becomes a cipher, just an example of a woman who breaks the rules and rocks the boat. They lock into a set of stereotyped roles and a number of ritualised interaction routines so that they can deal with her with a minimum of true involvement. The particular role an individual adopts and the rituals imparted reflect his or her habitual patterns of coping with the unusual and frightening. The pattern of relationships possible is established by the roles chosen. The de-individualisation of the quiet rebel severely limits her freedom of action. She may be precipitated into a number of totally undesirable roles and rituals. In the interests of predicting what is likely to happen, the quiet rebel needs to know something of the repertoire open to her co-workers and herself.

Extensive interviews with women at work, both rebels and non-rebels, have allowed the development of a taxonomy of the roles men and women use in these contexts. The list is, doubtless, not exhaustive. It may, however, be useful, because it crystallises the benefits of the experience of many women. The taxonomy is presented below in three sections: roles used by men; roles used by women; and roles offered the quiet rebel.

Roles Used by Men

The roles adopted fall into a number of discrete categories. Frequently, a man will only be capable of evincing one type of role; occasionally he can shift roles according to circumstances. Swift role changes are unlikely, because the role initially adopted normally represents the man's preferred mode of dealing with the threat posed by the quiet rebel. The fact that men do not often show chameleon powers is important. It means that having once categorised the role a man chooses to perform in relation to oneself, he becomes more predictable. The more predictable he is, the more manageable he becomes. So, the rule of thumb is: classify, predict and control.

HUSBAND, FATHER, SON

Faced with a quiet rebel, many men find themselves without any directly relevant past experience of dealing with women in a similar capacity. The relationship is novel. Their usual manner of relating to co-workers may seem inappropriate, so they have no ready-made model for their interactions with her. Often they resort to importing into the workplace a model they are familiar with at home. They act out the role of husband, father or son.

The actual choice of role will depend on the relative ages of the man and quiet rebel concerned. Normally, if he is older, he dons a fatherly persona; if he is younger, he prefers the part of son; and, if they are contemporaries, he may try husbanding.

The interesting aspect of this evocation of family roles is that it may generate sympathetic parallels in the quiet rebel. She too, after all, has to work out what to do in her relationships with male co-workers, and she too might feel safer if she could import well-learnt and trusted roles from the home and hearth. To his father, she plays the daughter; his son, she mothers; and to his husband she becomes a wife. The inherent complementary of these roles represents a real pressure to conform. It is almost like the knee-jerk reflex; he bangs the spot marked daughter and up she jumps.

Of course, these three roles each focus on different types of interpersonal demands and duties. Each has a combination of rights and obligations attached. The Father figure is empowered to instruct, direct and punish, but has to protect and help too. The Son can legitimately expect support and lenience, but has to make repayments in respect and, possibly truculent, obedience. The Husband may call for caring, concern, and confidences, but must contribute backup strength and solidarity. These are only examples of what the costs and benefits of each role might be. The rights and obligations of the roles will be negotiated to some extent afresh by each person who inhabits them. The precise prescriptions will depend to a large degree upon what past experiences have taught him these roles should look like. Their execution will depend upon the quiet rebel satisfying her part of the putative bargain. It is difficult to carry on fathering someone who insists on mothering you. There has to be some consensus as to the script which they will perform.

Many women, rebels or not, report how irritating and frustrating they find this process of recasting them as mother, daughter or wife in the workplace. Most of them go to work to create a new identity for themselves which is not based on the family and feel trapped into recreating family patterns at work. The process is particularly harrowing when relations in their real family are not good. When a woman has had a poor relationship with her father, she may find the fact of another man taking that role releases many of her feelings about her own father, and the co-worker who tries to demand she acts as a dutiful daughter may find himself reaping the torrent of emotional upheaval sown by her father. In stark contrast, the male colleague who acts as son may find himself swamped by a maternal affection that was never satisfactorily deposited on her real child. If he is foolish enough to try the role of husband, he had better be sure that the lady has not just finished an acrimonious divorce.

If she allows the import of this network of domestic roles into the workplace, the quiet rebel can expect to be disadvantaged. Firstly, they are tainted with unwanted emotional clutter. Secondly, they place her, almost without exception, in a subordinate position, because women most frequently have less power than men in the family. Finally, they allow the men involved to cloak her real status and the changing role of women in the workforce. The tactics she can use to disrupt this neat little package of roles are the same as those she should use to sabotage other role networks, and they are described later.

JOKER AND GAMESMAN

The Joker and the Gamesman are not at all similar, except in their effects. The Joker, having recognised the quiet rebel as a serious threat, will do everything to avoid taking her seriously. The Gamesman sees the threat and launches into a campaign of oneupmanship. Both aim to embarrass, disconcert and belittle the quiet rebel.

Jokers use various forms of humour. The experienced Joker

will try out the full range on a woman to discover which makes her squirm most and then harp on that with excruciating regularity. They can be practical jokes: the removal of important tools or equipment from workbenches so that deadlines cannot be met; the substitution of false information so that effort is wasted in going to the wrong place or doing the wrong thing; or the unpleasant surprise (the unexpected important visitor, the cockroach in the desk drawer) sprung on the unwitting. These jokes have the dual purpose of unsettling the woman and making her appear less competent. They are often formulated as 'tests'. Skilled manual workers may steer close to the managerial wind to 'test' female apprentices. The young woman will be sent on fool's errands to the stores to get non-existent machine parts, or given an assembly job with central components omitted. It is a 'test' in two respects: will she pick up on the error rapidly, and will she take it all in good part. Proving your own sense of humour in the first 'test' may obviate the tendency for repetition. But the Joker may continue the treatment long after the rest of the men have established more sensible relations with the quiet rebel.

He may also use more varied tactics. He may tell jokes, as opposed to the use of practical jokes. Telling jokes may work at two levels: he may tell them to the quiet rebel, or he may tell them about her. The effect of telling them to her will depend upon the type of joke and the way she feels about it. Any Joker worth his malicious salt will choose an area which makes the woman uncomfortable, threatened or even outraged: the target is to unsettle her, and any negative emotion will do. With a young inexperienced woman, the natural target would be jokes playing upon sex. The problem facing the woman is convoluted. Even if she finds the joke amusing, unshocking, or just downright tedious, she has to decide whether she should show it. If she is not embarrassed by lewd jokes, she may be concerned about the conclusions the men might come to about her own character. If she is embarrassed, she might not wish it to show, fearing they will consider her prissy or childish. The Joker succeeds in putting her into a no-win situation.

By telling jokes about her, whether behind her back or not, the Joker can make her into a target for ridicule. He can attach to her, in the minds of the other men, ideas which would otherwise never have occurred. He can insinuate that she got her job only by sleeping around; he can label her frigid because she is known not to sleep around; he can query whether she prefers women anyway. The focus on sexuality is noted by most women. It is not surprising; sex, after all, is what divides her from them. If she is also separated by status, this can be a secondary target for attack, through jokes which emphasise the incompetence of all women and her by association.

Such jokes have their optimum ill-effects when the woman who is their butt knows of them but cannot confront them. They are quiet whispers and group laughs that rustle just after she passes. They are intangible enough to evade any rebuttal, which would just add to their credibility, but strong enough to change the way the woman is regarded and treated. She knows about them, so she is likely to change too.

Rumours dressed up as jokes are more easily digestible and more rapidly transmitted. Most important for the man occupying the role of the Joker, the fact that what he says is labelled a joke makes him virtually immune from counter-attack. Jokes are socially acceptable pieces of overt prejudice. Humour is one of the major lubricants of all forms of discrimination. This is evidenced by the way a great spate of jokes directed against an enemy will appear as soon as a conflict begins. More generally, people can get away with saying things in jokes which would never be permitted otherwise. The Joker consequently has considerable power.

It is tempting for the women concerned to reciprocate in kind; not so much by a direct counteract, but by removing the initiative from the Joker and indulging in a gentle bit of self-ridicule. She caricatures her own weaknesses and limitations, instead of waiting for him to do it. She, thereby, steals his thunder, his barbs lose their pointed edge because they are no longer novel. This means that she can mute the Joker, and her self-criticism is unlikely to be quite as damaging or as incisive as his would have been. She might not get off scot-free, but she minimises her injuries. It is all well and good so long as she does not get carried away by her own act. She might be inveigled into extending her repertoire and becoming a substitute Joker, commentating on the weaknesses of others with paining wit. This is to be avoided at all costs. It only results in the quiet rebel being ghettoised: trammelled in a limited role fulfilling a thankless social function.

Where the Joker's efforts against the quiet rebel require the collusion of an audience, the Gamesman plays alone. His aim has awesome simplicity: he wants to win in any form of comparison between himself and the quiet rebel. His tactics are less simple. They operate according to four central rules:

1.   He chooses when they will compete and what they will do.

2.   He determines the rules of the competition and changes them at any time to suit his own interests.

3.   He will redefine whatever happens to his own advantage (if he falls flat on his face, he'll say it's all part of a greater plan).

4.   He will close a competition if he feels his own defeat is imminent and never acknowledge it ever started.

The Gamesman has impregnable arrogance, matched only by his ignorance of how other people tick. He should represent an irritant rather than a major problem, because his games can be made to fool no one but himself. The quiet rebel pestered by a Gamesman must simply ensure that his machinations are public knowledge. Publicising them should be done with a certain cool dignity rather than with any show of anger. The last things the quiet rebel must do are to try to compete on his terms or justify her actions to him. The Gamesman should be given no food for self-aggrandisement.

Obviously, in some work contexts, competition with a Gamesman will be required as part of the job. If there is no way of ducking out, the quiet rebel has to be ready to be undercut and overridden, translated and misinterpreted. Her best bet is, firstly, never to act purely spontaneously with relation to the Gamesman but always to muster time to analyse his plot, and, secondly, to ensure that the rules of the game are publicly posted before battle begins, so that any later reneging is provable.

Women who have reported dealing with a Gamesman emphasise that he is continually looking for any emotional or skill weakness. Having discovered one, he works to magnify it. The most telling counter-attacks have resulted from turning his methods back on him. Watch for his foibles and fears, manipulate the competition so that it focuses upon them. Avoid patterned repetitive responses which he can develop defences against. Use novel assaults at unexpected times.

The Gamesman is a difficult character to deal with because he has probably had years of practice in the use of his tactics against other men. He is just shifting his focus of attack to the quiet rebel. If he has a number of enemies about from past encounters, the quiet rebel would do well to engage in coalitions with them. An orchestrated rejection of his value system and techniques might just disable him.

The descriptions of both the Joker and the Gamesman are admittedly rather bleak. The metaphor for their interaction with the quiet rebel is that of war. This may be overstated; in some instances the Joker and Gamesman roles are adopted more as a means of self-protection against the unusual rather than in order to attack it. The Joker's jokes and the Gamesman's game may occasionally be produced because the men concerned do not know what else to do. They deem both to be harmless. It is clearly important for the quiet rebel to differentiate these from the more deadly variants and treat them accordingly, ensuring that they remain harmless.

THE INVISIBLE MAN AND THE AUTHORITARIAN

The Invisible Man is so put about by the presence of a woman doing the job that he pretends for all practical purposes that either he does not exist for her or that she does not exist for him. The Invisible Man may be shy, retiring, and so embarrassed at having to cope with the quiet rebel that his reaction is engendered by the desire to escape. He cannot withdraw in reality and so, instead, he withdraws behind psychological shutters. Most women will recognise the Invisible Man type from other realms of their lives; he is the same chap who would never approach an unknown woman at a party yet watches her every move discreetly, almost slyly. At work his fear can be frustrating and obstructivist. It may mean that the quiet rebel cannot work effectively with him at all, or not until she has peeled away the sheets of his reserve.

The Authoritarian is equally obstructivist, but for different reasons. He feels it is his God-given duty to uphold the letter of the law. He relishes refusing to do anything above or beyond his specified tasks, and loves to catch others in the act of some impropriety. On first entering a workshop, office or organis-ation, the quiet rebel may find the Authoritarian the earliest opponent. New to the place, she is unfamiliar with the system and its regulations and represents an easy target for the sharpshooting Authoritarian. He is the quickest to tell her that she has used the wrong procedure, she has not got the right clearance for certain forms of information, she does not dress in a manner suiting her position, she should have got prior agreement for petty cash expenditures, she really is not contributing enough to the 'family spirit' of the department, and so on, *ad nauseam.*

Psychologists have suggested that authoritarianism, what some people call the peaked cap mentality, is a stable and dominant aspect of an individual's personality. It tends to combine with other characteristics: excessive fear of and respect for those with greater authority; a disproportionate delight in the exercise of one's own authority in trivial demands; a tendency to conformity; dogmatism and rigidity in attitudes; fear of novelty; political conservatism; and moral immaturity. Some have argued that this syndrome is a product of the person's family background: a feared father and subjected mother.

This knowledge may help the quiet rebel to deal with the Authoritarian, especially upon initial contact. For a young woman, he may be a shock—although she is likely to have come across authoritarians at school or in training. She needs to bear several things in mind. Firstly, he treats everyone this way, and she should not feel personally to blame when he attacks. Secondly, most of his threats of dire consequences for misdemeanours can be totally ignored. Thirdly, when she wants something done fast, she should bypass him by going to his superior or by using informal channels. Fourthly, Authoritarians do not garner much sympathy, so when in trouble she should get other people to back her up. Finally, she can play upon the Authoritarian's fears. She can invoke the power of higher authorities or the force of company law to gain sway. She can play down the novelty of any suggestion to push the thing past his vigilant rejection of change. She can even manipulate his dogmatism and moral immaturity to her own ends with a little careful planning: evoking his most categorical beliefs to support her plans.

The Invisible Man and the Authoritarian both have the power to obstruct the quiet rebel. They require quite different coping strategies: through repeated encouragement the Invisible Man may actually be brought to visibility; the Authoritarian is a lost hope, he is unalterable and simply has to be manipulated in any way that proves effective. It is worth saying that dealing with either is very stressful and frustrating. The effort they require cannot be minimised. It may be flippant to say that the key to success lies in keeping the disruption they generate in proportion, but it is nevertheless true. It is too tempting to over-emphasise the importance that these men can have. Perhaps, perceiving them as fearful and fallible helps adjust the way they can be treated.

THE MALE CHAUVINIST, THE MALE FEMINIST AND THE EGALITARIAN

The men occupying the roles described so far are really pussyfooting around the prime bone of contention: the fact that the quiet rebel is doing 'men's work' in a 'man's place'. There are a set of roles which focus upon this very fact: the Male Chauvinist, the Male Feminist, and the Egalitarian.

The Male Chauvinist is undoubtedly the most renowned. Originally, chauvinism was the label given to bellicose patriotism, after Chauvin, a Napoleonic veteran, in the Cogniards' *Cocard Tricolore* (1831). In time it has come to mean offering fervent support for any cause. At its simplest, male chauvinism is represented by aggressive adherence to the belief that men are superior to women and should be dominant. It is an interesting sign of the times that some men now feel the need to proclaim this view where in the past it would merely have been taken for granted as true—not just by the majority of men, but by women too. In an important sense, male chauvinists are a product of the shift in the relative power of the sexes. Overt male chauvinism is a response to the need to resist change. Superiority which is challenged has to be defended.

Male chauvinism may not be recognised as a social movement, like feminism, but it has a strong central ideology. This is a system of beliefs which are set up to justify male dominance economically, socially, and politically. It suggests that women are inevitably inferior, due to their biological and psychological make-up. Women are less logical, more emotional, and doomed to child-rearing and domestic incarceration. The beliefs are backed by misinformation and distortion.

Male chauvinists come in at least two sizes: the Pig and the Closet Pig. The Pig is circled by an entire folklore of his own now, and there is even an industry producing Male Chauvinist Pig artefacts (ties, badges, tee-shirts). The Pig makes no secret of what he thinks; he tows no feminist line. He is rude and aggressive, and he drains every ounce of machismo from any dealings with women. He suggests that women love to be dominated and tries to prove it. He mouths all the old adages about a woman's place. He litters his life with dissatisfied and angry women, but never listens long enough to hear what they think of him. He is like a torpedo cutting through the sea, deadly and self-destructive. Yet the Pig has a standing as an anti-hero. Men who for one reason or another cannot emulate him, admire in him the resurgence of manly 'virtues'. Even women will acknowledge that with him they know where they stand.

The Closet Pig is a different breed. He is the man who holds to all the male chauvinist beliefs but secretly. He is too afraid to live openly according to his beliefs. They, consequently, sneak out on those occasions when his guard is down. People around him get to know about his attitudes gradually, because they insinuate themselves into his actions and preoccupations. But the Closet Pig will not defend his views when challenged. They only get expressed clearly if he feels supported in a group of like-minded men. Then, he allows his prejudices full play.

The Pig at least flies his true colours; the Closet Pig does not even have that saving grace. The former can be tackled directly; the latter protects himself from any direct contradiction. The psychological dynamics of the Pig and the Closet

Pig are quite different. The one revels in notoriety and the challenge to conventional social etiquette; the other is afraid of revealing his real self. Both may fear changes in sex roles, but the one capitalises on it to make a counter-attack and slow those changes, while the other cringes away unless given leave for prejudice by an accepting climate.

The quiet rebel is the incarnation of the changes which both types of male chauvinist fear, and she can expect the full frontal attack from one and the knife-in-the-back from the other. Many women have wasted a lot of energy over the last two decades trying to reform and rehabilitate male chauvinists. Anybody deciding to do this should weigh the costs and benefits first. If they can be ignored rather than treated, they should be. Argument with the Pig is pointless, because he is not interested in facts; he already knows you are illogical and driven by emotionality, and will not hear you. Argument with the Closet Pig is impossible because he will not admit to his real opinions. Ignore them, do not rise to the bait and you deprive them of their sport. By all means ridicule them if that relieves your tension, but never make the mistake of taking them seriously. There is nothing more irritating to the Pig than being treated as a buffoon—it does not equate with the macho image. Some of the interaction rituals described below illustrate how to explode the Pig's inflated ego. Pigs are particularly open to the disruption tactics considered because they rely heavily on predictable interaction gambits.

The Male Feminist is another role which can be used. It may sound like a contradiction in terms, but it is meant to label a man who claims sympathy with the feminist cause. Most often it will be a self-proclaimed label. The man will claim to believe that women have been subjugated and should be given equality of power and opportunity. He will reject his allegiance to the male oppressors and identify himself with the struggle for change.

Whether the man's self-professed conversion is genuine or

not, can obviously be queried. It is noticeable that such claims are most frequently heard from upper-middle-class intellectuals, and the sincerity of their motives may be complexly related to reality. After all, why should a man align himself with a movement that is contrary to his own interests? It could be argued that his only motive is altruism: helping others selflessly. It could be argued that equality of the sexes is, in the long term, in his interests, because it will free him to do many things which are denied him now. It could be argued that his protestations are cynical attempts to curry favour and evade the guilt of past oppression. In fact, every claimant to the title of male feminist will have his own motive, and it is quite important to discover it before trusting him.

Some feminist groups would argue that a man can never be a feminist. Being feminist requires the experience of having been sexually oppressed, the consciousness of powerlessness and the unity with other women which that evokes. Such groups would deride attempts by men to claim understanding and would shun their offer of support. Support from men would, they argue, merely recreate dependence on them and the loss of self-control.

For the quiet rebel, in the workplace, offer of support from a man claiming sympathy with feminism is attractive. Before accepting it, she needs to be sure of his motives, especially if she has no particular allegiance to feminism herself. Find out what he means by feminism, and whether he translates his feelings into action or is it all just talk. Is it all a glib act meant to ingratiate or put you off guard? If it seems as though it might be, it is sensible to avoid self-disclosure to such a man. Do not tell him how you feel about feminism or your place at work. You may find this is just he wants, information on your doubts and fears which will give him greater power over you. Self-disclosure is an important component of the development of relationships, and the quiet rebel has to learn to control it and do it only when appropriate. We will return to this in later chapters.

The Egalitarian is a role described by many women. Egalitarian may be a misnomer; potential egalitarian may be more precise. This is the role occupied by the man who is genuinely trying to come to terms with changes in sex role expectations. At home, he tries to do his fair share of all household chores. At work, he tries to shake off preconceptions and prejudices built on stereotypes. Sometimes he succeeds, sometimes he fails. His failures are bred of ignorance or habit, not malicious intent.

The Egalitarian is plotting a course as new and dangerous as that charted by the quiet rebel. He is discarding lessons learned as a child, shedding whole skeins of self-protection, and looking with unblinkered eyes at what his fellows have done in the past. He has a right to feel confused and unsure. He is an adventurer in an emotional wasteland, and he has to build new ways of relating to women that are not founded on inequalities of power.

Recognising the Egalitarian can be a problem. Bitter experiences may canker the way the quiet rebel views all men at work. Cynicism may blind her to real attempts by a man to be egalitarian. She may interpret them as efforts after ingratiation, tricks, ploys, anything but genuine attempts to treat her as an equal. When he falters in his efforts, this is taken as proof of his covert intentions. A sort of paranoia sets in, and the quiet rebel finds it difficult to believe that any man is not part of the institutionalised sexist conspiracy.

This sort of thinking is self-reinforcing. Trusting no one, you never get fooled; it pays off, so you carry on mistrusting everyone. You live behind the barricades under a self-induced state of siege. Healthy psychological functioning requires that the barricades be mobile. You have to sample the outside air, even at the possible cost of some wounding.

When it looks as though a man may be an Egalitarian, he needs to be given a chance. He needs to be educated: shown what you need from him and what you are willing to offer in return. In the workplace, what you might need from an egalitarian manager might range from an equal chance to talk in meetings to access to the same clients, or from training opportunities to heavier responsibilities. If you have a supervisory role in relation to the Egalitarian, you might wish to show him the ways in which he can most aptly comply with instructions, or the differences between your management styles and those of male counterparts. In offering this education and an opportunity for him to develop as an effective egalitarian, the watchword has to be innocent until proven guilty. Only after he flunks several chances should you assume he is a no hoper. That way, you avoid paranoia, but the line is ultimately drawn and you do not waste too much energy. That way, you avoid exhaustion.

In mentioning exhaustion, it is important to recognise that frequently the quiet rebel will be dealing with a number of men enacting a series of roles. In a single office she may have the Male Chauvinist, the Father, and the Joker. Dealing with them is like decapitating the Hydra: rid yourself of one head and another takes its place. No coping strategy will make them go away. The best the quiet rebel can do is to minimise the damage they inflict by manipulating them quite consciously according to sound psychological principles.

Her progress may be both hampered and accelerated by the other women in the workplace.

Roles Used by Women

MOTHER, DAUGHTER, WIFE

Just as some men lock into familiar domestic roles when dealing with the quiet rebel, some women use mother, daughter or wife roles. It is probably true to say that these would be the roles that they would employ in relating to a male occupant of the quiet rebel's job. They do not need to revise their chosen roles, though the strains of their execution may be different. This arises because they are no longer performing their Mother act opposite a son, or the Daughter to a father, or Wife to a husband. When two women are involved, the Mother finds a daughter, the Daughter a mother, and the Wife a strange spouse. The fact that they no longer face the male counterpart to their role changes the whole tenor and outcome of the relationship. The obligations and privileges of the roles change. For instance, a daughter, as played by the quiet rebel, makes different demands on a Mother than would a son: she would be expected to be more responsible, less reckless, more caring, etc., than a son. This revision of the rights and duties evoked in the interaction may be unwelcome. It certainly requires a change in habitual patterns of dealing with life at work.

One solution to this problem adopted by some women when dealing with the quiet rebel is to push her into the masculine counterpart of their role. For instance, it is a commonplace to say that the secretary of an executive is his office wife; she performs the same caretaking functions at work that his wife does at home, sometimes down to sexual gratification, though not as often as novelists would have us believe. Secretaries dealing with a woman boss may find that initially she does not expect to be quite so cossetted and serviced. They may find she shows a disconcerting egalitarian streak: she makes her own coffee, she explains why certain jobs have to be done rapidly, she invites comment on decisions made, and so on. In short, she dams the smooth flow of the stream of authority. Female executives report how they are re-educated by their secretaries, who show them what they should expect to have done for them and who are disdainful of attempts at independence. Once they overcome the incongruity of being skivvied for by another woman, many find having a wife a wonderful thing. They would like one at home as well as at work.

The quiet rebel dealing with Mother, Daughter and Wife figures at work has to decide how far their perpetuation is to her advantage. She may find the Mother's support, the Daughter's dutifulness, and the Wife's backing valuable props. Alternatively, she may find her energies are being diverted into wasteful attempts to maintain the false images of herself which may be involved. Each quiet rebel has to make her own value judgement. If she wants to break out of the role system, she can. She simply has consistently to fail to conform to role expectations. If she is cast as daughter, she refuses to comply with role requirements: she does not show patient regard for her 'Mother', she does not follow her advice, and so on. Any system subjected to such disruption cannot survive long.

BITCH AND SUPERBITCH

The Bitch is a staple product of any work environment. She is normally in her forties; though some are early developers, it is really a role for the mid-life crisis. She is usually well-packaged: she makes the most of her looks, which are not phenomenal, and of her figure, which is a little the worse for wear. She has a hot-line to the rumour-manageress, a tongue that can cut glass, and wit enough to make her snide jokes both revealing and painful. She would cut your throat as soon as smile at you, and when she smiles icicles form in the bowels of the fainthearted. She has no real friends, though she will engage in transient alliances as long as they offer benefit without personal cost. She seems to believe that the rest of the human race is her enemy, and by the time she is through, she is probably right. Superbitch has all of these qualities plus some.

Superbitch is a little bit more clever. She operates where money and power are concentrated and is intent on getting as much as she can of these vital commodities. Her motto is 'Look out for yourself alone'. All opposition is steam-rollered by whatever means is available; the more underhand they are, the more success is relished.

The quiet rebel will meet the Bitch and Superbitch at all levels of the organisation for which she works: as her subordinates, peers, and bosses. She will probably find herself a special target for attack because she may threaten the primacy of Bitch or Superbitch; also, she is in a particularly fraught position and they love easy prey.

Some of the self exercises described later in this book actually suggest that the quiet rebel should practice some of the techniques employed by the Bitch and Superbitch so that she can adopt them at will in self-defence. Observing them in action is consequently valuable, as long as you are not crushed in the process. There seem to be a number of rules of thumb to remember in developing a defence which can be derived from what women in these situations report. Firstly, never ally with a Bitch unless you are desperate, and then only if you can benefit even if she pulls out and leaves you in the lurch. Secondly, avoid giving her any information about your private life and minimise any about work. Thirdly, watch her carefully. Finally, do not hesitate to keep her in check by using the authority vested in your job.

THE GOSSIP

Categorising this as a woman's role is really sexist. A man can do the job just as well and as often. The Gossip is the relay circuit for work rumour, and rumour is very important. Psychologists have studied how rumours operate and found that they serve clear social functions. Rumours can appear to arise out of thin air: suddenly, everyone is passing on the rumour that a takeover is imminent or large-scale redundancies are due. In fact, rumours reflect the central preoccupations of the group generating them; they come not from thin air but from the fears, doubts and wishes of the people mouthing them. Most often, rumours start with some slender fragment of fact which is then elaborated upon and distorted to confirm the major concerns of their audience. For instance, the firm's managing director is reported to have a hurried meeting with the bank manager. From this small acorn many rumour oaks can grow. The firm is bankrupt, the firm needs capital to expand, the firm is due to join a consortium, the director's wife is having an affair with a bank clerk, and so on. The acorn which takes root will be the one which is closest to the needs and fears of the firm's employees. The other thing to remember about rumour is that it is passed on by word of mouth. This means the story gets changed slightly with each retelling: each tongue licks it further into shape with its own idiosyncratic rendering. The rumour might start with a simple statement that the firm needs capital, but by the time it reaches maturity it might state that the firm needs £3 million over two years for retooling in order to capture a new Middle East contract that will mean staff increases and a restructuring of middle management. Each contributor to the rumour bends it a little in the direction of his or her special interests. A rumour has a sort of organic growth pattern.

Once loose in an organisation, a rumour is as difficult to control as a plague of locusts. The dominant rumours can set the tone for the entire workplace: redundancy rumours can stunt productivity growth; rumours of mergers can produce panic withdrawal of funds, etc. The longevity of a rumour and its power to upset the balance of the workplace ambience depend very much upon how close it is to the central concerns of the majority of people working there, and upon how far it can be countermanded by fact.

In controlling rumour, the Gossip can be central. The Gossip roots out rumour like a pig finds truffles. She can smell the pungent odour of ripe rumour and, once she has it, she transmits it to all and sundry. Of course, the juiciest rumour is that which concerns intimate personal details, particularly of those with any authority. The hint of scandal means a rumour that few can resist. Where there is no hint, the professional Gossip might feel obliged to invent – just to keep her clients happy.

The quiet rebel has to expect to be a focal point for rumour. She is breaking the rules, she arouses fear and envy; so she is prime material for rumours which will find elaboration in the emotions she initiates in colleagues. Rumours can, obviously, be damaging. If she finds herself rumoured to be someone's mistress, or repeatedly incompetent, or a man-eating slave-driver, she may legitimately feel insulted and unjustly attacked when she is none of these things. The potential that such rumours have for damage can be minimised by the use of a number of tactics. The first involves tedious repetition of the truth in face of the rumour. This assumes that you are aware of the nature and content of the rumour. The second entails monitoring your Gossip, so that you know what rumours prevail, and feeding into the system judiciously chosen titbits which deflect her from yourself. This tactic of establishing counter-rumours can be enjoyable, as long as you are not already too upset from the discovery of the original. The third tactic is to allow the rumour to run its natural course without allowing yourself to respond emotionally. This means analysing what is happening before permitting yourself the luxury of a spontaneous reaction. Such restraint requires practice. In using all of these tactics, it is necessary to remember that rumour is a social product controlled by social processes. The Gossip may be a fount of rumour but she is not truly in control, so you will not avoid being the butt of rumour by attacking the Gossip. Take advantage of her instead. As a general rule, the quiet rebel has to remember that social processes cannot be halted, but they can be used to her own ends.

THE FLIRT AND THE TRAMP

The Flirt and the Tramp are complex personality types and differ considerably. The Flirt rates herself as attractive and sets out to attract. She is confident of her own sexual power and likes to exercise it. She likes to be firmly in control: she issues the come-on and she determines the pay-off, if there is to be one. She uses her flirtations indiscriminately to get her own way in trivial things. Her ploys include claims to helplessness, gentle self-exhibitionism, and wordy badinage full of *double entendre*. She likes to think that men are putty in her hands.

The Tramp could be said to be a flirt who has paid off too many times. She is known as a soft-touch by the men she works with, and any attempt to fight against her reputation is desperate. The Tramp is often characterised by the women around her as a sad victim rather than being deemed to be in control. Putty turns to steel in her hands.

For the quiet rebel, the Flirt and the Tramp may be an irritant rather than any real problem. Mostly, she will be immune to their charms. She may find their effect on male co-workers annoying, but a live-and-let-live attitude seems most effective. Trying to tame or reform either could be considered presumptuous and time-wasting.

FANS AND GROUPIES

Fans and Groupies are roles women can take up which have specific relevance to the quiet rebel. Sometimes the quiet rebel will discover that the women with whom she works will regard her with awe because she is actually engaged in rebellion. They think her wonderful, a special exception, and tell her so. Often but not always this occurs with older women, who see the quiet rebel doing something they never had a chance to do. Where the Bitch might resent her achievement, Fans and Groupies admire it and wish her well.

There is a tendency, however, for them to go overboard in their paeans of praise. They over-estimate how unusual she is and how much she has achieved. Their reasons are varied: they would probably like what they say to be true, because it would mean that they should not blame themselves for not having done what she has done; she is exceptional and cannot realistically be expected to be emulated. This interpretation of their exaggerated praise is supported by the fact that frequently, in the same breath, they will claim that they would have done it but they never had a chance.

Fans and Groupies are surprisingly difficult to deal with. They can praise you to embarrassment. They can expect too much from you and, when you fail, you feel the sharp pain of their disappointment. Being put on a pedestal may be fun as long as you are not asked to dismount unassisted in a hurry. It is best not to allow the pedestal to get too elevated from the start. A little reality therapy is in order. Fans and Groupies should be disabused of any false ideas about the extent of your success as soon as they appear. Short-term losses in ego-boosts will be amply repaid by long-term gains. You will not continually have to struggle to fill some unrealistic ideal they have of you.

Roles for Rebels

In talking about the roles that the quiet rebel can play, it is necessary to distinguish between those which others seek to impose upon her and those she would choose for herself. Most of those described here are of the first sort. Some come into being as reciprocations for roles enacted by others (like the Mother-daughter, Husband-wife chains), while others are elaborated from stereotypes of atypical women which have developed in the working community.

QUEEN BEE

The role of Queen Bee is reserved for the quiet rebel who makes it to the top; normally she is the first woman to do so in her organisation. She is deemed to have determination and single-mindedness and, above all, she is hard. She is hard to please, hard to beat, and hard to understand. She is an exacting taskmaster to herself and to anyone who works for her. She makes no concessions for weaknesses and expects everyone to work as hard as she does. She is dictatorial: she makes the decisions, others are supposed to obey. She crushes opposition or competition as soon as it rears its head. Consequently, the major emotion surrounding her is fear.

Her central philosophy is simple: the only way to succeed is through superhuman effort and self-control. She, therefore, has no brief to help other women struggling to follow in her footsteps. In fact, she merely sees them as threats to her own uniqueness and prospective challengers for her power. She is just as likely as a male manager to discriminate against them.

This 'Queen Bee syndrome' was first labelled by social scientists in 1973, but it had been part of managerial folklore for many years prior to that. The question is whether women who gain success do normally respond in this way. It seems from research on successful women executives that the truth may belie the image. Women managers in the 1980s claim that they are keen to foster the development of other women in their organisations. They fancy the role of mentor, and few consider themselves fearful figures to their subordinates. How far these claims represent reality is unknown. It may be that successful women now know that they are expected to nod in the direction of sisterhood. They also know that becoming a Queen Bee is isolating and stressful. The role is surrounded by a sense of criticism. Being Queen Bee is not socially acceptable, so they reject the role on the surface, but the sense of insecurity and will to win which generate the Queen Bee syndrome are likely to remain beneath the surface. Consequently, women who claim to be benign dictators may be simply fooling themselves or those who listen to their protestations.

The quiet rebel set up as Queen Bee by colleagues has to weigh the costs and benefits. The benefits are manifestly increased power: people fear her more and are more likely to respect her demands. The costs include the stress of isolation, the need to operate independently of social support, and the requirement for continued and ever greater successes. The Queen Bee cannot afford to be seen to fail. She erects an image of herself as indestructible and infallible—if the image crumbles, her power dissipates. Before accepting the role of Queen Bee, the quiet rebel has to decide whether she is willing to shoulder the full burden of its implications. To some extent, these spread into her private life. Perfection at work is supposed to be paralleled at home. She is supposed to be able to rear her family and run her house impeccably, and to be disdainful of any woman who finds this impossible. She is thought to organise her domestic arrangements with clinical and military precision. It is tempting to see the role of the Queen Bee as that of an ambitious, aggressive, automaton. The quiet rebel may or may not find this clockwork figure appealing; it is a matter of personal taste.

It is, however, worth remembering that the Queen Bee is effectively only an unattractive caricature of what may be essential for success in a competitive world. It is instructive to consider that men who are successful also behave in the ways so unpleasant when attached to the Queen Bee. What is acceptable practice for the gander is here pathologised (labelled a syndrome, as if it were a medical complaint) in the goose. Avoiding being typecast as a Queen Bee may mean the quiet rebel actually eliminates from her tactics things which are fundamental to success. This is clearly a mistake.

The most adaptive strategy seems to entail neither identification with nor rejection of the Queen Bee role. The quiet rebel needs to feel free to use her aggression and pursue her ambitions without feeling chained to them in perpetuity.

THE TOKEN WOMAN

The quiet rebel will immediately recognise the Token Woman role. As long as she remains the sole woman in her organisation doing her job, she will be plagued by this role. It works in a number of ways. As the Token Woman she is assumed to represent all women. This means that she is expected to respond in any situation as a woman first and as an engineer, shepherd, electronics wizard, or whatever, second. Queries are addressed to her 'for the woman's perspective'. Since this is often done in a way which implies the woman's perspective is second-rate and unnecessary, continually being asked to mouth generalised views, and not ones which may be relevant but non-female, becomes irksome.

Being the Token Woman also means an obligation to be supergood at the job. You are told in no uncertain terms that all women will be judged by your performance. If you fail, half the human race will be failures. If you succeed, there is a chance that they will employ another woman in your type of work.

Being the Token Woman often means being regarded as inferior in some respects to the men doing the job. The Token Woman is told that she is there not because she has the necessary skill or talent, but because she is a woman. The criteria for admission to the work have been relaxed to give women a chance to enter it. Positive discrimination in favour of women has had the spin-off effect of devaluing the achievement of many women in gaining access to men's work without its help.

Refusal to play the tokenism game is problematic. It is

difficult to win either way. You offer views as a woman, and you are criticised for thinking only in terms of gender; you refuse to offer the 'female view', and it is never voiced. You claim your failures are your own, and it is treated as a cover for general female incompetence; you succeed and attribute it to women generally, and you are deemed too modest and your achievements unique to you. You show that you have ability in the job equal to anyone else who does it, and you are considered a freak example of positive discrimination's success; you fail and their worst prejudices are confirmed, even if you were initially as qualified as anyone for the job.

The solution may be to allow tokenism to run its course and stick to your own. Ultimately, tokenism can only be overcome by more women gaining such work. The task of the quiet rebel is simply to succeed; her very existence increases the likelihood of more women joining her. She acts as a model for them and a precedent.

Tokenism may be a thorn in her flesh, but it is important that the quiet rebel does not allow it to engulf her or determine her actions. She has to express both her own views and the 'woman's perspective', and she should not be kidded into believing that through her all women are judged, or allow her achievements to be deprecated in her own mind by smears of positive discrimination. Dealing with tokenism is a matter of deciding how it works and of seeing through it to the motives which drive it and the silly ploys upon which it depends.

BLUE STOCKING AND OLD MAID

The Blue Stocking and Old Maid roles have a lot in common and are more widespread than might appear at first glance. The Blue Stocking is generally recognised as clever and serious; she does not need to be especially intelligent or academic, she simply has to read a book or two and speak with respect of the world of ideas. There is a strong anti-intellectual tradition which makes being a Blue Stocking rather unfortunate. People think that they cannot communicate with her, that she is unsociable and not interested in romance and similar super- ficial fripperies. This isolation can be modulated if she has knowledge which people need. She then becomes a sort of walking reference book, the swot who does everyone else's homework.

The Old Maid similarly has her uses. She is cast in the role because she shows no signs of sexual contact with men. She is assumed to fear men and sexuality. Often she has an old relative dependent upon her, and so is a figure of pity. She is also someone to turn to for nurturance and support. She provides the back-up at an emotional level that the Blue Stocking offers intellectually. No one thinks she minds being the workplace nanny, because they believe she finds in it an outlet for her thwarted maternal instinct.

The quiet rebel may find herself being channelled into these roles if she has any of the defining characteristics. In some ways, either can be rewarding, as in both you feel needed and grudgingly respected. However, the quiet rebel who adopts either role may have to deny whole realms of her personality and whole cadres of her needs. If she does not wish to do this, she must disrupt the process which attaches the role as soon as she sees it arising. The putative Blue Stocking must show that she is interested in people as well as ideas and is not omniscient. The potential Old Maid must register her desire to be independent and her need to be treated as a sexually-responsive woman. Early disruption of the process means that measures to show its inapplicability can be small-scale, but once the process is in full swing, the disruption tactics have to be more dramatic. The late response is dangerous, because you may need to deny aspects of your self which are very important but need to be denied in order to evade the role.

THE RABID FEMINIST

The label feminist when used as an insult carries a multitude of connotations. It reaches its fiercest when prefaced by 'rabid', since this conjures up the image of the infectious madness of a rabid dog. The quiet rebel, no matter how blithely apolitical, is bound to be labelled a feminist at some time, for her ambitions and achievements embody much of what feminism is popularly considered to be about. But the Rabid Feminist role may not fit her at all.

The Rabid Feminist is characterised by fanaticism: un-reasoned, indiscriminate aggression against men; paranoid delusions of male conspiracies against women; total rejection of her own femininity. The Rabid Feminist role has no relation-ship in truth to any extant feminist group or belief system. It is a conglomerate of all extremist views ever expressed as part of feminism, filtered through a sieve of fearful male prejudice. The Rabid Feminist is attributed with all sorts of socially un-desirable characteristics: she is foul-mouthed, dishonest, illogical, vicious, sexually perverse, and so on. One can almost hear the call: 'Lock up your daughters, there's a rabid feminist on the loose.'

This monster image of the feminist is clearly a product of fear and is also an attempt to ridicule to the point where any sane woman would not wish to be labelled feminist. The quiet rebel has to be wary of being moulded at work into a Rabid Feminist. Even mild expressions of feminism can be magnified, taken out of context, and treated as proofs of the infection. Speedy counter-attacks are essential: identify who is the main person spreading this image of you and tackle him (or her). The best way seems to be to expose what they are doing publicly and to explain that it is bred of fear, envy, gamesmanship, or whatever. The strategy is designed to sow seeds of doubt in other people's minds about the validity of the image while simultaneously warning off the main offender. But it is important when disrupting this Rabid Feminist attribution not to run away from some of the characteristics associated with it. Fearing to be indicted as Rabid Feminists, some quiet rebels withdraw from assertiveness and the public statement of their beliefs; this is, or course, just the sort of response that is desired by those who typecast. The quiet rebel who distorts her own behaviour and beliefs is allowing herself to be controlled by the role just as surely as if she was acting it out. She becomes a photo-negative of the role, and those characteristics in her which evoked fear are consequently curtailed. The quiet rebel cannot afford to let the role control her in this way. Knowing the role, she still has to attempt to be herself, untouched by it.

Beyond the Roles

The taxonomy of roles used by women and men and imposed on the quiet rebel is not exhaustive. The roles described are simply those which women themselves most frequently talk about. They are described here as illustrations of what the quiet rebel might find awaiting her in a man's work. Forewarned is forearmed.

With this in mind, any quiet rebel needs to analyse her workplace carefully. She needs to identify which roles are being performed and by whom. She must catalogue the rights and duties attaching to each role so that the actions of others become more predictable and, if she chooses, more manipulable. Where roles not described above are being enacted, she needs to observe their characteristics and guess at the motivations and needs which underlie them. She must be aware of the roles that are being pinned to herself, and take care not to become typecast.

The process of typecasting acts to de-individualise and thus constrain freedom of action. The quiet rebel should resist this.

Roles are imposed to control, and the quiet rebel should be in control of herself. She should be sensitive to attempts to mould her into some prefabricated shape that is more amenable to existing belief systems and practices. She will not be able to stop the process being initiated, but she can disrupt its course. Instead of casually donning the role proffered, she should show publicly its inadequacies and its constraints. She has to remain independent of the role structure: a free agent roaming within it. And one of the most fundamental ways of disrupting the typecasting process is to disrupt the rituals which support it.

Interaction Rituals

Interaction rituals are interchanges between people which involve a fixed repeated pattern. Like religious rites, they require solemn observance. If he says this, then you are obligated to say that. Deviation from the expected form causes consternation and confusion. The ritual can involve more than two people and can comprise deeds as well as words, feelings as well as beliefs. Rituals are used to cement social relationships: the evening-long ritual of the dinner party, for instance. Rituals are used to minimise personal investment in a relationship; its production requires limited thought and no imagination. Rituals are tied to roles: for instance, the 'dumb blonde' is expected to generate inane comments that can be made to look stupid. Rituals consequently form a link in the chain of social control which binds the quiet rebel. Scratch the surface of a ritual and it bleeds social rules and regulations.

Interaction rituals that comprise gambits of social control over the quiet rebel are varied. Only a few need be mentioned to give an idea of how they work.

'Isn't she attractive when she's angry?' This is used when you are in the middle of an argument and are about to launch a withering onslaught that is bound to prove you right. It is a

form of disorientation tactic, which distracts you from the main point and, immediately, brings your sexuality to the fore. It is as if you are seen to be angry in order to make yourself attractive, and the point of the argument is superfluous. The comment defuses the ammunition you were about to launch. It simultaneously implies that your anger is only acceptable because it is deemed to be part of the flashing-eyed beauty act. It effectively warns that your anger is really inappropriate. The use of the comment becomes part of an interaction ritual if the woman who is its butt always responds in the same way: with heightened irritation, confusion, blushing, silence, or whatever. An habitual response means that she is liable to being controlled; it can always be used to generate confusion, silence, and so on.

"But you are exceptional . . .' This is used when you are in the process of having a success not normally associated with women. It is often used by women Groupies or Fans, but is sometimes also used by men. You then have the choice of bigheadedly acknowledging your uniqueness, or denying and deprecating yourself. Either way, it is one of those no-win situations. Often, whichever way she responds, the ritual requires that the woman is challenged. If she says she is exceptional, her interlocutor will remember other similar cases. If she says she is not, this will be vehemently denied. She ends up by having to defend herself for having succeeded. Just the sort of ritual to reverberate with any residual fear of success she might have.

'I don't mind women but . . .' This is normally followed by an extended diatribe against women which is said to stem from what other people think. The woman on the receiving end has to listen to the abuse but is prevented from attacking the source, since he has denied his own responsibility before beginning. When she defends women, he says coyly that he could not agree more. It is like stirring porridge with a feather: he is immune to altercation.

'*It is true that a woman's place is . . . though, isn't it?*' This usually comes from the 'little-boy-lost sexist'. He pretends his sexism is all bred of genuine naïvety and gives the impression that he might learn better if you invest a bit of time and effort in his education. The ritual proceeds when you do try to tell him about women and find that he never does learn. His naïvety is just a cloak for blind cynicism. The problem is that over numerous repetitions, with other women besides yourself, he has refined his technique. He knows which questions cause the maximum self-doubt and prove most traumatic for women. Again, the little-boy-lost image protects him from a direct retaliatory onslaught . . . until you recognise the tactic.

'*What's the matter with you anyway?*' This requires the quiet rebel to justify her unusual work. At first it might appear to be a genuine attempt at understanding; it becomes ritualised when the person posing the question refuses to accept as truthful any answer you give and chooses to impose a preselected interpretation on your behaviour.

Everyone will be able to identify the rituals that they are most frequently asked to act out. The ones which people continue to use are those which suit their own interests. People find themselves trapped into the same old battles, founded on the same pattern of initiation and counter-responses, because it serves those with whom they battle.

Interaction rituals work to control the quiet rebel for two reasons. Firstly, they are effective because they are designed to disarm by playing on self-doubts, guilt, anger, fear, and so on. Their usage is refined by frequent replays, so that they focus minutely upon the optimal emotional reactions. Secondly, they work because the people initiating them are working to a formula which they do not need to consider, but the recipient is off-balance, having to work out the best response possible given that previous responses have proven unproductive.

Faced with this dilemma, the quiet rebel needs to disrupt the ritual. She has to work out what rituals are most harmful to her.

She then has to decide how she has been responding to them in the past and engage upon a deliberate campaign to vary her responses. She has to monitor under what conditions the ritual normally occurs, and go into them with a plan of action worked out in advance. Whatever then happens, she needs to stick to her plan. It does not really matter if her actions seem totally irrelevant. The object is to disrupt the ritual; if irrelevance achieves this, it is appropriate.

In choosing how to respond, one rule of thumb is useful: do not respond meaningfully to the surface ritual, respond to the underlying message. So, when he says you are beautiful when angry, tell him you know that he is trying to side-track you to stop you scoring a point, that he is showing tell-tale signs of being threatened, and that he'd better watch out. This analytic tactic, where you turn amateur psychologist, can be infinitely confusing, especially when the analysis is totally incorrect but serves the purpose of disrupting the ritual. The task then becomes to ensure that this response does not become part of a new damaging ritual.

The quiet rebel can develop interaction rituals of her own which act as tools of self-defence. She can resort to them when unsure of what to do or say. Each quiet rebel has to tailor her own defensive rituals to fit her particular context. The one who is being labelled a Queen Bee might routinely indulge in 'the pratfall': she might self-consciously make minor errors that a subordinate can rectify. Psychologists have found that people with power who make minor errors and acknowledge the help of others become more attractive and persuasive in the eyes of others. As long as the ritual is not too visible or overtly artificial, it works, in this case, to humanise the successful woman executive and fend off the Queen Bee image. The woman labelled a Rabid Feminist might wish to counter-attack with a ritual in which she retaliates by calling the man in question a Male Chauvinist Pig. She turns a one-sided attack into a genuine slanging match with insults flying both ways. Done with some semblance of humour and lashings of hyperbole, this can point out how ridiculously exaggerated his claims about her actually are.

The use of self-defensive interaction rituals can be immensely valuable to any hard-pressed quiet rebel. They require less emotional energy than spontaneity, they have more impact, and they counteract the demands of workplace roles. They do, however, require cool calm thought about what is happening. They can only be developed after the quiet rebel has carefully analysed what it is she dislikes about something that is habitually happening to her and has decided what needs to be done to change the cycle.

Analyse Relationships

At the kernel of this chapter is the assumption that the quiet rebel has to analyse the nature of her relationships in the workplace. She has to be aware of the network of roles which surround her and sensitive to the rights and obligations attached to them. She has to be able to predict what other people will do on the basis of the roles they perform, and ensure that her own freedom of action is not constrained by roles that others try to impose on her. She has to monitor interaction rituals and be willing to disrupt them in order to control roles attributed to her. The way to achieve good working relationships requires three steps: observation, analysis, and, only then, action.

Further Reading

Tropp Schreiber, C., *Changing Places*. Cambridge, Mass.: Massachusetts Institute of Technology Press, 1979.
Cooper, C. and Davidson, M., *High Pressure: Working Lives of Women*

Managers. Glasgow, Fontana, 1982.

Cavendish, R., *Working on the Line*. London: Routledge and Kegan Paul, 1982.

Staines, G., Tavris, C. and Hayaratne, T. E., 'The Queen Bee Syndrome,' C. Tavris (ed.), *The Female Experience*. Del Mar, Cal.: CRM Books, 1973.

Chapter Five

SEXUAL HARASSMENT

The Lecher was omitted from the catalogue of roles used by men in the workplace only because he deserves special and separate mention. The Lecher is typically portrayed as finding it impossible to relate to a woman as anything other than as an object of sexual gratification. His sexual advances are indiscriminate and mostly grossly inappropriate. Caricatured as a dissolute, fornicating, old bore, the Lecher has become a figure of fun, ridiculed by men and women alike. He is a pitiable phantom somehow made harmless by the hilarity that surrounds stories of his unsuccessful amorous escapades. Folklore seems to do a whitewash job on the Lecher, but his harmlessness is a mirage, there only in retrospect. In reality, he is a nasty piece of work. The irritation and dismay he causes the women who are his prey is both long-term and damaging.

The existence of the caricature also serves to make the Lecher an eccentric. He is pictured as an exception, as if it were odd for a man to treat women as erotic footballs in the game of sex. The caricature distracts attention from the run-of-the-mill sexual harassment of women which is institutionalised in the workplace. Lechery is not the preserve of one unusual type of man: the Lecher reifies the activities of most men.

Forms of Sexual Harassment

It is only in the last ten years that the extent of the sexual harassment of women at work has been finally appreciated. For as long as the patriarchy has existed, it has gone unlabelled and denied. Now it is recognised to occur with unfailing regularity in all types of workplaces. Even trade union leaders and industrialists now speak openly of its prevalence where previously they refused to admit any knowledge of it.

Sexual harassment refers to unsolicited and unreciprocated sexual advances which assert a woman's sex role over her role as a worker. Sexual harassment can take many forms: the laying on of eyes, hands, and other organs, not to mention words. It can be restricted to careful staring at your legs or intent gazing at your left breast. It can progress to pointed comments on your appearance, your clothes, your posture, which move into questions about your private life, queries about your romances or sex life, and the recounting of pornographic jokes. These constitute verbal nudge-nudges and winks. Words may give way to action. Clinches and pinches in any secluded spot; a casual pat on the bottom or swift stroke of the nipple in a crowded lift; a stolen kiss or jocular hug; all constitute harassment, if unwanted. Of course, it can be taken further, with explicit attempts at sexual favours that range from invitations involving euphemistic dirty weekends to rape.

Often the sexual advance initially appears without fore-warning; there is no gradual build up as in courtship. It can be fleeting and ambiguous. The women involved can hardly believe that they are right in interpreting a comment as sexual innuendo or the incongruous embrace as a sexual approach. They doubt whether they understand what is happening. They wonder whether they would be right to rebut something which might not actually be there. Yet, at the same time, they feel discomfited and, somehow, violated. All forms of sexual harassment seem to evoke this sense of outrage. The initial doubts give way to certainty when the advances are repeated. Experienced women workers can identify the onset of harassment without hesitation; their outrage is more deeply ingrained and laced with cynicism.

Every working woman can describe her own favourite or worst incident of sexual harassment, but it is not something which is commonly or openly discussed. Women seem to have joined the conspiracy of silence about it. This can be partially explained by looking at why sexual harassment occurs and the consequences it has.

Reasons for Sexual Harassment

The most straightforward explanation for the phenomenon of sexual harassment is also the most naïve. It would postulate that it is all just part of the natural mutual attraction between the sexes. Men are, according to this explanation, just pursuing their normal inclinations and, since everything natural is good, their actions are justified. For such an explanation to hold water, it would have to be proven that harassment was a product of sexual arousal. In fact, too few men are willing to admit to behaving in such a way to know whether they find it an erotic stimulus. The evidence from women to the contrary is, however, plentiful. They do not find it arousing, and there is absolutely no reason to believe that when they say this they are lying deliberately or unconsciously. Harassment is experienced as stressful, anxiety-making and threatening, emotions not usually compatible with sexual pleasure. Women subjected to sexual harassment describe how it makes them feel insecure in their job, less competent, and less in control of themselves.

Women's responses to sexual harassment may offer a clue as to the real reason for it. Sexual harassment is a particularly effective way of denigrating and controlling women. In the case of the quiet rebel, this may be very important. Women who aspire to men's jobs challenge society's notion of their sex role, so what better way to return them to their proper place than by emphasising their sexuality over and above their status as workers? Women in men's jobs challenge the personal power of those men with whom they work, so what better way of reasserting that power than by taking every chance to emphasise their sexual subordination and vulnerability? The real reason for sexual harassment does not lie in amorous desire, but in the struggle for power at work. It is a game of dominance in which the decks are stacked against the woman.

Penalties for Playing the Game

Since sexual harassment takes many forms, it is difficult to generalise about how the game is played. Much will depend upon the status of the man and woman involved. Nevertheless, it is probably true to say that the woman has a number of discrete options open to her. She might pretend that it is not happening. She can do this by choosing to reinterpret events in such a way that they lose their sexual significance: the sexual banter is seen as friendly chat; the roving hands as fatherly reassurance; and so on. She can only realistically manage to do this for the lesser forms of harassment, and even then she is likely to persuade only herself. But it is stretching the imagination too far to pretend that rape or serious assaults have not occurred. Once events have reached that sort of pitch, reinterpretation is not feasible. Yet even then the matter can be treated as a shameful secret, and the woman may refuse to face up to what has happened. Recent research has shown that women are afraid to report rape, especially by men known to them, because they fear that they will not be believed or will be blamed for 'leading the man on'. Women can, through fear, come to collude in their own sexual mistreatment. By refusing to tackle harassment publicly, they allow it to continue. They are playing into the hands—if the pun is forgivable—of their oppressors.

Cloaking harassment in mists of silence and denial will not make it go away. Instead, it is likely to result in its accentuation or escalation, for two prime reasons. The man, finding he can get away with one level of harassment, will see whether his luck holds good when he tries something more serious. Moreover, if the real reason for harassment is to assert male power over women at work, it would not be serving its function if the woman were able to ignore it. If she could ignore it, it would be failing to show her that she was the object of male sexual gratification. Escalation to the point where it cannot be ignored is the only answer in such circumstances if harassment is to fulfil its purpose. Women who seek to ignore it, fail to understand the dynamics controlling harassment. The men concerned do not get gratification from the sexual advance itself, but from the emotional turmoil it engenders in their female target. If she evinces self-control and a placid non-chalance, they need to go further to achieve their gratification. It is possible, that finding the tactic initially unrewarding, the man will go elsewhere for his power fix, but this is a gamble and the woman has to take it only after calculating the real risk of escalation.

One young woman who tried the denial tactic with her employer describes what happened: 'He used to come and talk to me about things irrelevant to the job, my personal life, my boyfriends, and would claim that I did not smile enough at work. He said he liked to see me smile. He pestered me to smile whenever he saw me and would stroke my cheek until I did. I began to feel like a pet animal. So I resisted. Then he suggested I might like to go out with him and he would make me smile. He was married, and I did not find him at all attractive. I refused to go out with him. He caught me leaving the office late after I'd been going over some papers and cornered me at the end of the corridor. He kept asking why I felt I was too good for him. He started pushing me around. I got away and did not return to the office but resigned. I had done everything I could to ignore his pestering, but it just got worse.' This pattern of escalation is a frequent occurrence.

An alternative option open to the woman instead of ignoring the harassment is to enter the game as a fully-fledged player. The woman can self-consciously choose to use her sexual allure to her own advantage. She can set out to tempt, charm and win over her male colleagues. She can offer sexual favours, whether real or illusory, as carrots at the end of a long road of compliance and hard work.

As one retail manager said: 'I know I'm attractive and I know that I can get what I want by using it. It charms a man's vanity to feel he is attractive to a woman who is attractive. It is nothing more than that. I make them feel good and they feel obligated. Sometimes they expect too much, but most of them just want to be admired. It costs me nothing.'

There is no doubt that there is a venerable tradition of women using sexual manipulation to their own ends. Whether this ultimately gains them power or puts them into subordinate positions is debatable. Many feminists would argue that this sort of sexual payment for services rendered merely simultaneously exemplifies and perpetuates women's powerlessness: if they had power they would not have to depend on sexual Machiavellianism; since they do, they cannot wrest anything other than transient control. Such control is based on sex drives which are too variable to be constant. Moreover, such control is tenuous, since there are other women in the market offering sexual competition. If she does not have sole control of the sexual commodity market, a woman who relies on it is in an uncertain position.

In any case, the woman who responds to sexual harassment by attempts at manipulation has two fundamental problems to face. Firstly, she misunderstands the cornerstone of harassment. Harassment is not about allure, it is about dominance and control. The woman who seeks to take the initiative away from the man is contravening the rules of the game. The harassment loses its point if the woman, far from being upset and embarassed by it, actually directs and enjoys it. This implies that a woman may use sexual manipulation with men who do not attempt harassment, but with those who do it is unlikely to work in predictable ways.

The second problem centres on the changes that will be wrought in her work 'persona' if she actually allows herself to become sexually involved with men at work. Compliance with their sexual demands can directly result in a loss of her 'character'. She comes to be thought of as promiscuous, morally lax, an easy target for other men, and so on. She acquires a sexual reputation that can mean that she is heaped with scorn by men and other women. Sometimes the sexual reputation is acquired after a genuine relationship with a man for whom she has a real affection breaks down. The wolves are soon at her door, suggesting that they are no different from the other fellow, so why shouldn't she satisfy them? By that stage, she is on a vicious treadmill. All illusion of being in control or manipulative evaporates, and she is trapped. The game is lost.

Some women seek a totally different option. They try to evade the game. They do this by attempting to neuter themselves, not literally, but by removing the overt signs of their femininity. This process of de-sexing oneself involves serious efforts to eliminate outward signs of one's existence as a sexual being. The woman deliberately makes herself unattractive by her choice of clothes, hairstyle, make-up and so on. She avoids talking about her personal life, and she studiously avoids conversations even touching upon romance or sexuality. She ensures that there is no hint of flirtatiousness in her gaze, actions or bearing. She will resist any social contacts with male colleagues. Her self-presentation is, in sum, asexual as far as that is possible.

This strategy is clearly bred of the belief that it is a woman's own attractiveness or action which lead to sexual harassment. If harassment is designed to achieve dominance, there is no real reason to believe that it will be deflected by a woman's attempts to de-sex herself. It will occasionally work because a man can be made to look perverted or silly if he harasses a very ugly woman. The dominance he earns is thus moderated by the censure that flows from other men. Yet still the woman does not win. She makes herself unattractive and strictly curtails her normal range of behaviour to avoid sexual harassment, only to find that she is liable to ridicule and pity because she is handicapped in the sexual game. Such pity and ridicule can be as demeaning and emotionally disturbing as sexual harassment itself. The woman still finds her self-esteem, freedom and respect limited.

All three responses to sexual harassment seem to carry unpleasant and unavoidable penalties.

Penalties for Refusing to Play the Game

In a game where you cannot win, the sensible thing to do is to refuse to play. Often, however, women cannot exit the sexual harassment game because the penalties for refusal to take part are too great. The woman who will not play her part is open to a number of attacks. If the man has higher status, he can arrange it so that her conditions of employment are less favourable. He can refuse her overtime opportunities, insist on bad working hours, impose injurious job transfers, or shift her to less amenable tasks. He can manoeuvre her into loss of promotion or even demotion by rigging her job evaluations. He can prevent her gaining a new job by providing her with unsuitable references. He can organise it so that her job performance is so bad that her dismissal is justified or her life so miserable that she resigns. If she remains and steadfastly refuses to respond to his sexual advances, she is subject to a whole battery of verbal abuses which attack her sexuality.

The problem in defending oneself from these penalties centres on the fact that they will not be overtly tied to the refusal to comply with sexual demands. It is difficult to show how loss of promotion, and so on, are directly related to an unwillingness to allow wandering hands or to pander to a voyeuristic curiosity with salacious confessions. It becomes especially difficult when the sexual demands are covert, implicit, or ambiguous, occurring swiftly and, perhaps, identifiable only in retrospect.

Women feel that there are no formal channels which work to offer redress for such grievances. They feel that they cannot prove their case and tend to remain silent. Most women seek to 'ignore' sexual harassment rather than responding to it one way or the other. They think that by 'ignoring it', by pretending that it is not happening, it will go away. This is normally a temporary phase, since it does not go away. Ignoring it merely serves to accentuate it. No response is treated as encouragement and silence as passive acceptance. Frequently, women will not even speak about their experiences to other women workers, feeling that they would be censured for 'leading the man on' or that, if they have a higher status than the other women, they would lose their authority. The social norm which directs women to compete for men's attentions in this case operates to prevent them acting as a group in their own best interest. Women can actually be the worst critics of a woman who refuses to play the game when they feel they are already trapped in it. Mutual suspicion is antithetical to mutual support, and there can be spitefulness in communal defeat. In the end, women are often driven to quitting.

Women who cannot cope and resign are actually removing themselves from the sphere of competition. They damage their promotion prospects and, probably, in times of economic recession, their chances of ever gaining employment again. This is, of course, all to the advantage of the men who stay. So, sexual harassment can have two advantages for men: firstly, it denigrates the women with whom they work and reduces their competence; secondly, it can eliminate women who might otherwise be direct competitors.

The Sexual Double Bind

A double bind is the name given to a problematic situation where there is no simple correct response. In a double bind, any response entails penalties. Sexual harassment places the quiet rebel in a double bind. It is damaging for her either to resist or to submit: it is a dilemma where whatever she does is wrong. But this should not be treated as a counsel of despair. Although no individual strategy seems useful, collective strategies can work.

Women in the workplace need to pool their resources to deal with sexual harassment. The range of strategies feasible varies with the type of harassment operating and the number of men involved. Although sexual harassment is institutionalised, in the sense that it is the norm in most workplaces, there are often only one or two main culprits who have to be put out of action to make life more bearable. When these use the lesser forms of harassment — suggestive talk and touching — a series of steps might help in the containment of the problem. The first step entails the woman victim doing a *cognitive reappraisal* of what is happening. This involves her seeing the sexual approach as an attempt to dominate her and not as a genuine expression of lust. Taking this new perspective on events is not easy. It requires a certain persistence, and is facilitated if the woman can calmly gauge her own initial emotional responses. If she felt demeaned and out of control rather than sexually excited, she might more readily conclude that it is a game of dominance that she has involuntarily joined. This first cognitive reappraisal is an important step in preventing the onset of self-blame and self-doubt which eat away at self-esteem and confidence. The woman has to understand that she did not initiate the harassment, she should not be ashamed to admit that it is taking place, and she should not be fooled into believing that any social censure to accrue would fall on her. In fact, the longer she remains silent and isolated, the more likely she is to be deemed responsible. As one woman said, 'The longer I kept quiet the more guilty I felt. It was as if I was his confederate. I know the other women had seen what was happening, yet they said nothing. It was as if I had to give the signal for it to be officially recognised. The more hesitant I was, the more they thought I wanted it. Some even seemed jealous; they envied me the attention. I wish I'd done something as soon as it started.'

In dealing with harassment, the woman should make what is happening known to other women. In doing so, she is most likely to discover that the majority of them are having similar problems. She comes to understand from this that she is not unique and that her difficulty says next to nothing about her as an individual.

The third step is rather more difficult. It entails achieving some sort of agreement with the other women on how to tackle the harassment. Negotiating a united plan of action and getting everyone to work in concert requires great determination. The woman who takes on the organisation is too easily victimised as a troublemaker. Motivating women to repel harassment may prove difficult too because they fear reprisals. In some cases, it is possible to lead them into action by example. Any effort which meets with success is likely to be emulated, and initial successes can be built upon gradually so that ultimately much more risky tactics can be employed and will be copied by other women.

The woman who does this is deliberately taking on the role of ringleader. If she also happens to be marked by other women as a quiet rebel, due to her choice of job, she can find she has a simultaneous advantage and weakness. The advantage lies in the fact that they already expect her to be nonconformist: the disadvantage stems from the fact that they do not closely identify with her. The quiet rebel has more degrees of freedom in dealing with sexual harassment, but she will also have less of a following.

The best way to encourage women to resist sexual harassment is probably to give them very specific things that they should do in particular situations. They need to be helped to work out in advance how they will respond when an habitual advance is made. The object, as in the case of the interaction ritual, is to disrupt the flow of the sequence by doing the unexpected. Every woman has to identify the characteristic stages in her own harassment for herself, but a few examples might help.

The Public Endearment One type of sexual harassment involves a public show of intimacy which has no foundation in reality. The man uses terms of endearment (darling, sweetie, dear, and so on) to the woman in front of other people; he sits too close to her, infringing her personal space, in public places; he implies in conversation with others that she confides in him; all of this amounts to a declaration of intimacy. The irony is that this is purely for public consumption. When they are alone, the performance is dropped and their relationship is impeccably straight. The woman faced with this is in a dilemma: she knows people are getting a distorted message about her, but any open rebuttal will seem to blow the thing up out of all proportion; if she tackles him in private, he can deny all knowledge of it and claim rightly that their relations are perfectly bounded by propriety. His tactic can be disrupted, however. His patter can be interrupted deliberately in a number of ways. The woman can reciprocate directly in kind, matching endearment for endearment in a most supercilious way. Alternatively, she may make a semi-humorous remark about the way he calls all his junior executives dear and follow it by pointing out that she is the only one who is female. Whatever she chooses to do, she has to remember that she has two audiences: the man who harasses, and his public. If she can gain the sympathy of the latter, she is depriving the man of his pay-off. He is unlikely to continue with a line of attack that is unrewarding. This may not mean that his harassment stops completely; it may just shift its focus, but the first battle is won.

The Sexual Interrogation   This type of harassment normally occurs without an audience. You are meeting for some totally ordinary work matter and suddenly he pops in a question like: 'How is your love-life these days?' 'Are things all right between you and your husband/boyfriend?' 'Don't you find sex is uppermost in everybody's mind now?' and so on. Taken by surprise, there is a tendency to reveal more than one would wish, but more than this the curiosity is frequently just prurient. The questions throw you off balance, distract from the business in hand, and shift you out of a working relationship to something more intimate and less defensible.

In coping with sexual interrogation it is important to remain calm. Keeping embarrassment and anger in check will enable you to think faster. As a general principle, the best response seems to be to mirror the question. If he asks how your love life is going, do not answer; instead, ask him how his is doing. Mirroring can disrupt the ritual just enough to provide you with an opportunity to calm down and reconstitute work thoughts. If it fails, it is important to avoid making personal revelations. Find an excuse to leave: remember a non-existent appointment, hear an imaginary telephone bell, anything to give you time for cool reflection on what needs to be done.

The Wandering Hand   The best deterrent for the chronic pincher, squeezer and feeler is a broken wrist, preferably meted out by accidentally dropping something heavy. Failing this, embarrassment tactics can be used: a cry at full volume, which attracts everyone's attention, that he's at it again, can dissuade the most ardent. Humour tied to rumour can be particularly persuasive. The wandering hand can be made a laughing-stock by the retelling of carefully edited stories.

The tactics used in these examples will only work if the woman concerned can gain some support, preferably from other women but even non-offending male colleagues will do. The isolated women who tries to employ these tactics will be open to all of the penalties mentioned earlier. If the tactics are used in concert by all the women affected, reprisal becomes unfeasible.

The quiet rebel is clearly especially vulnerable to sexual harassment and least likely to gain social support, particularly if she is the sole woman working in a firm. She may need to be assiduous in cultivating the friendship of male colleagues in alliance against the harasser. If that is to work, she has to prove herself valuable and honest, so that her protests against the harassment are believed. She is, after all, working against a multitude of sex-role stereotypes and has to maximise her persuasiveness. Some of the techniques for doing this are discussed in Chapter 8.

The more serious forms of harassment may not be amenable to treatment even with cohesive collective responses. Sexual blackmail, when sex is extorted under threat of the sack or worse, and rape require legal action. The woman has to make use of the defence that the law provides and should use any prop *en route* — her union, her overall employer, and so on. No excuse for failure to use the law is justifiable. This may sound a harsh judgement, since action may mean job loss and a smear campaign against the woman's morals. Yet it is the only tenable course of action, since silence means the bitterest form of sexual slavery. In taking appropriate action, the woman may need help. This is increasingly available from Rape Crisis Centres and from other counselling agencies. The woman requiring accurate information and emotional sustenance should go out and get it. The quiet rebel has to remember that she can go beyond the workplace for a network of support. She does not have to operate in a vacuum; she should seek help whenever she needs it and wherever she can get it. There is no intrinsic value in standing alone. Even where the help offered is of no practical use, the sheer existence of support is known to minimise the psychological ill-effects of stress of all sorts.

The Societal Response

The ultimate death-blow to sexual harassment can only be meted out when societal attitudes change. As long as sexual harassment is deemed in some sense normal and the women involved are treated as responsible for it, it will continue. It is questionable whether there is really the public will to change these attitudes, for it is in the interests of large sections of the powerful shapers of attitudes, in the media and civil service, to restrain women through sexual fear. The fear constrains women's freedom of action: it makes certain places taboo; certain jobs are black-balled; certain times of night are curfewed. The woman alone knows that she is a legitimate target except when she restricts her activities and timetable and location to those permissible under an unwritten code. Women who flaunt the code are not only likely victims, they are also considered to be culprits; they are blamed for their own victimisation. The need not to be alone, the requirement for a male protector, may no longer be founded on economic pressures, but it is still prevalent.

In claiming that societal attitudes to sexual harassment will be slow to change, a caveat is needed. Societal attitudes are not some ethereal entity. They are comprised of what individuals think and feel, and we each contribute to our society's attitudinal ethos. Societal attitudes can be shifted by changing our own attitudes and those of the people close to us. The ripple from the small stone cast into the middle moves out to all corners of the lake. The impact of individual attitude changes is cumulative.

There is particular value in starting this change within your own family. Women subject to sexual harassment often explain that they are too frightened to tell their husband or boyfriend. They fear that it will erode their trust, encourage suspicion, feed their desire to return the woman to the domestic sphere, and possibly cause a violent attack on the man concerned. This fear results in silence and again cuts the woman off from potential support. It seems very important to educate the men in one's family about the facts of sexual harassment at work. They will know about it from the male point of view from their own experiences; they need to be told about it from the woman's perspective. Any preconceptions about it being pleasurable or amusing or good clean fun should be smashed, repeatedly if need be. It is always best to assume that such re-education requires frequent repetition and subsequent refresher courses. It is all too easy for the man to forget again when he is re-immersed in the macho mythology of the workplace.

Any power that the quiet rebel has to change the attitudes of other people rests upon her ability to clear her own mind of misconceptions first. Her primary responsibility is to prevent herself from being conned into believing that she benefits from the sexual harassment game, that she initiates it, or that she should be held to blame for its outcomes. She should not be lulled into passivity by tales of the magic charm of her feminine wiles. Feminine wiles are an invention of men offered as a consolation prize to the women they dominate. Use your feminine wiles, they say, and you can have the crumbs off our well-stocked table. It's an offer almost equivalent to asking the ravenous dog to beg for its bone; not quite though, because at least the dog that begs gets the bone.

The quiet rebel who gains a clear understanding of the dynamics of sexual harassment has a tremendous advantage. She can plan her tactics in advance and can gather social support at work and at home. She may not be interested in joining any social or political movement which may finally embody changes in societal attitudes to the sexual control of women in legislation, but she plays her own part by making her personal struggle for freedom.

Further Reading

Farley, L., *Sexual Shakedown*. London: Melbourne House, 1980.
Smart, C. and Smart, B., *Women, Sexuality and Social Control*. London: Routledge and Kegan Paul, 1978.

Chapter Six
No-Go Emotions

No-go areas are normally the product of urban guerilla warfare. They are war zones which it is dangerous to enter and where only the foolhardy linger unless unavoidably detained. A parallel can be drawn with the world of the emotions. There are emotions which should be deemed no-go areas. These are the emotions of self-doubt, self-blame and guilt. All three are treacherous: they mislead and they immobilise you. Unfortunately, most women who break with tradition by taking what is commonly regarded as a 'man's job' regularly have to traverse these emotional no-go areas. They are faced with self-doubt, self-blame and guilt because of their job choice.

The important thing for the quiet rebel is to know how to navigate and negotiate through an emotional no-go area. The purpose of this chapter is to provide some of the essential navigation and negotiation skills.

Why are No-Go Emotions so Dangerous?

Everyone needs to feel that they are worthwhile or valuable in some way. Everyone likes to feel that they are making a unique contribution—that the world would be a lesser place if they had never entered it. We all need a positive image of ourselves. We all need to believe that our attributes, at least most of them, which make us different from others also make us worthy of respect. This is true whether the attributes concerned are physical (the shape of your nose, the colour of your eyes, the distribution of your subcutaneous fat); psychological (your phobias, obsessions or compulsions); or social (the groups you join, the house you own, the money you earn).

Fundamentally, we like to feel good about who we are. Whether we do or not largely depends upon systems of values erected by society over long periods of time, for society lays down which attributes are good and which are bad. We learn from the moment of our birth what our society deems good and what it considers bad, and we soon know whether the attributes that make us different from others are worth having or not.

Very sensibly people then try their hardest to play down or ignore attributes which society labels worthless, while simultaneously calling attention to whatever 'good' attributes they possess.

We all play the game of seeking to 'accentuate the positive, eliminate the negative' about ourselves, and it can be done in a number of ways. Take, for example, the woman who feels herself to be too fat. She sees in those around her a tendency to ridicule and pity people who are grossly overweight, and she hates being fat. She might try to diet. If that is successful, all is well. She gains a positive image of herself reflected from how others see her. If the diet fails—and they all too frequently do—she has to take other measures. She's fat and she gets no kudos from it. So she tries to get people to change their attitudes to her fat. She becomes the life and soul of the party: telling jokes about herself (e.g. 'When weighing scales see me coming they groan'). The jokes cloak her real feelings: while she's laughing at herself, she doesn't have to admit, at least not in public, her fear and frustration. The jokes can also make her fat amusing rather than ridiculous to other people. In so far as this is true, jokes can serve to make fat, or any stigma, socially

acceptable. Admittedly, the social acceptance is only temporary and transient, but it serves the needs of the moment and
gets the woman through another day.

The fat woman who becomes the joker takes one route out of
the trap which social norms and values have set her, but there is
another escape route. This entails the woman saying: 'Yes, I'm
fat and I know that is not good, *but* I have other characteristics
which mean that I am still worthwhile and I want you to
recognise that.' So she insists that people recognise her brilliant
wit, her green fingers, her organisational excellence. She directs
attention away from her girth to other things from which she
can gain a positive self-image.

Whether the woman chooses to capitalise upon her obesity
(no matter how superficially), or seeks to push it aside beneath
a plethora of alternative, more socially acceptable qualities, she
is actually negotiating a self-image and a social role for herself.
She accentuates the positive and eliminates the negative to
arrive at a satisfactory picture of herself.

It is time now to return to the original question: why are no-
go emotions so dangerous? Self-blame, self-doubt, and guilt are
dangerous because they sap your confidence, and confidence is
essential if you are to build and maintain a positive self-image.
All the work that you do to accentuate the positive and
eliminate the negative aspects of your self can only be pursued
as long as you have confidence. When confidence wilts, people
become more wary, less assertive, and lose their ability to
persuade others. If you have confidence in yourself, others have
confidence in you. Lose your confidence, and you lose their
confidence and your ability to manipulate the way others see
you and value you. The obese woman who tells jokes about
herself in a hesitant, unsure way only worsens her plight—
becoming an ever-more piteous figure.

The no-go emotions have to be avoided if you are to build a
valuable self-image. Remember we are all standing on a spiral
staircase which descends from security to despair. Each step

down we take increases the likelihood of our taking the next and the one after that and so on into the pit. Each loss of confidence we have makes subsequent losses more likely, because we have less left to carry on the business of rebuilding a positive self-image and thus restoring our confidence. It is a vicious circle and one in which it is easy to get enclosed. Escape lies in controlling the no-go emotions.

Why are Women so Subject to the No-Go Emotions?

Women are more subject to the no-go emotions than men on the whole, and from a very early age are more likely to indulge in self-blame and self-doubt. As was described in Chapter 3, the sex difference is evident by the age of four and continues throughout life. Women are more likely to feel responsible when they fail or when things go wrong: they take the blame and feel guilty, whereas men tend to attribute their failures to circumstances, chance, fate, indeed anything but themselves. The reverse is true where success is concerned. When things go well, men claim that it is all due to their talents, skill, hard work, or effort. Faced with success, women prevaricate. They claim it was just luck, things happened to pan out that way, anyone could have done it.

Put simply, men fear to fail; women fear to succeed. Unfortunately, this means that whatever happens women get a raw deal. If they fail, they blame themselves; if they succeed, they accept no praise.

Jane, a young woman training to be an engineering technician, exemplifies this paradox perfectly. Jane found her training interesting and enjoyable. She was good at the job, and her difficulties lay mainly with relationships with other workers. She was the only female technician in the firm, working with men who were twenty or thirty years her seniors and regularly made fun of her. The favourite way was to embarrass her by telling dirty jokes to each other in front of her. She would blush and they found this highly amusing. Instead of regarding this as symptomatic of the inability of the men to act sensibly towards her, Jane regarded it as her own fault. She believed that it would be solved if only she could learn not to blush when such jokes were told. She put it all down to her own inadequacies, blamed herself, and started to doubt whether she should be doing the job if she could not deal with these situations. Self-blame and self-doubt loomed large. In contrast, when told, as she often was, that she was doing a good job and mastering technical operations quickly, she would disclaim responsibility, claiming that it was all due to the fact that she had a really good supervisor and tutor. Consequently, she got only a minimal boost to her confidence when she was praised and a massive deflation of it when things went wrong.

Why do women clasp failure to themselves and hold success at arm's length? No one really knows exactly how this is brought about. Most frequently it is explained in terms of the differential socialisation patterns of boys and girls. Socialisation is the process whereby children are taught the central components of their culture by significant agents in their lives: parents, teachers, peers and the media. Girls, it is argued, are taught by their parents and at school to accept responsibility for their failures and reject responsibility for their successes. How? The cues are very subtle and not overt, but children are quick to seize on the meaning behind any obvious message. It seems that in various ways parents and other influential characters in the child's world lead girls to believe that it doesn't really matter if they fail—they are not expected to excel. The girl, realising this, is more willing to accept failure than her male counterpart, who is told it is very important for him to succeed. On the other hand, having been told it is not necessary for her to succeed—indeed that it might be positively unwise to do so, since it makes her less dependent and feminine—the girl who then proceeds to succeed will not accept responsibility for it.

In addition to responding to direct socialisation pressures, girls often have clear examples of how women should respond to failure and success in the adult women who rear them. Children model themselves on the adults who surround them. If mother is indulging in self-blame and self-doubt, daughter thinks that is the way it should be. Daughters are rarely carbon copies of their mothers, but they are also rarely completely fresh top copies.

Children are most assiduous observers of their elders. They see, memorise and repeat actions and emotions whose true meanings they come to understand only much later. They see with a vision undistorted by complex value systems and prejudiced preconceptions, and draw conclusions that have a clarity undiminished by exigencies. Daughters watch their mothers and formulate a conception of what a woman should be and do which is a direct extrapolation from them. They see what may be purely unintentional or automatic aspects of their mothers' actions or emotions as a fundamental component of womanhood. Mothers who habitually exhibit self-doubt, self-blame or guilt teach their daughters these are acceptable emotions without knowing they have done so. Indeed, since children have a tendency to idealise their parents, the mother who indulges in the no-go emotions may place them on a pedestal: something to be prized and admired.

One highly successful executive who administered the finances of a large firm described how she had for many years been ashamed to admit her numerical and financial acumen. She was embarrassed to be proven correct on decisions regarding money matters. She gradually came to realise that this was an habitual response which she had learnt from her mother, who had actually had charge of their family's small business but who had pretended that her father was the business-mind. She described how her mother would do the books in secret and become very defensive if asked about it. To outsiders, the father was the sole proprietor. Her mother acted behind the scenes efficiently, but without pride in her activities; in fact her pride lay in her capacity for self-effacement. It took this woman a long time to realise that she was modelling her own responses to financial management upon those of her mother.

The impact of unintentional modelling is important, since it may counteract things which a mother is overtly teaching her daughter. The manifest message may be full of epithets about equality and confidence, but if it is accompanied by a hidden agenda that tutors the no-go emotions it is doomed to failure.

Subjugation to the no-go emotions is passed on from one generation of women to the next: we learn our no-go emotions by watching others indulge in them, and get rewarded for accurate copying. Fortunately that does not mean that you have to stay subjugated forever or, indeed, that you have to transmit the yoke to your own daughters. The no-go emotions can be controlled. Some women already do it.

Breaking Tradition and the No-Go Emotions

When the quiet rebel decides to break with tradition and take a job normally done by a man, she enters an emotional minefield. The temptation to slump into the no-go emotions is great, and the reasons are simple. The woman is trying to ignore limitations and taboos which have been placed upon her actions from an early age. She is deciding to compete with men directly, on their terms and in their arena. She does not do, maybe for the first time in her life, what is expected of her, and she knows this will bring down censure. She sees that other people think she is odd. Even when other people do not think she is odd, she is likely to believe that they do. There is a touch of paranoia involved in any break with tradition. What matters is that she believes other people scorn her decision, are perplexed by it, or in some other way think she has done wrong. This is at the root of the slump into the no-go emotions, generating self-doubt, guilt and self-blame in turn.

Believing that others decry our actions leads to self-doubt. After all, our self-image is heavily dependent upon what we see mirrored back from those around us. When other people, particularly those who are important to us, look askance at our job choice, we start to wonder. *Mirroring*—shaping your self-image on what others think of you—is a natural process. We all do it. We are infinitely responsive to feedback, even when it is couched in subtle cues. For instance, studies of body language reveal that people are acutely aware of the meanings of posture and stance and will alter their behaviour accordingly. We read what others tell us, whether they use words or not, and we do it automatically, without consciously paying attention to the process. In this way we learn what others feel about us and allow them to change how we feel about ourselves. It only becomes dangerous when you are trying to break with tradition and consequently breach the expectations others have of you. Their feedback can then be negative and disruptive. Then mirroring has to be carefully monitored or else your self-doubt is inevitable.

One young woman, training to be an underground railway driver, illustrates this problem. 'I felt that I would be good at the job and did not see any reason why a woman could not be a driver. Yet I knew my colleagues and supervisors saw me as an experiment and did not expect me to be good at the job. Don't get me wrong. They were not nasty or openly prejudiced against me, but at times I felt I could see myself through their eyes and I was just not up to the mark. I started to see myself in that way too. I started to doubt whether I was really worth training. I lost a lot of confidence.' In Kirsty's case, the negative feedback from others did not drive her out of her job. She persisted. But it is possible to see how easy it would be to adopt an image of oneself as incompetent and worthless in such a situation. It is also easy to see how a young woman might feel paranoid in it and come to doubt whether what she thinks other people think about her is right. The quiet rebel has to be aware that her unusual position makes her hypersensitive to criticisms, overt or implied, from others, and she has to dampen her responses so that she does not over-react too much. Jean, who works in the print shop of a newspaper as a typesetter, reports how she fell into the paranoia trap: 'I was continually looking for snide meanings in every remark directed at me. I was silly because I just took everything as a personal attack and came to think everyone really hated me. It is so easy to lose perspective and think the whole world reckons that you are a troublesome fool. I got no support from what anyone tried to do.'

Mirroring can be positive occasionally. Many women describe how, given good feedback from their colleagues, they have felt themselves change. One architect in her mid-thirties said, 'On several occasions the senior partner made a point of commenting on the creativity of my garden designs and I found myself increasingly concentrating on them and even came to think that they were really original. I started to think of myself as having a particular contribution to make in that area.' Another older woman, working in senior management in an insurance firm, suggested that she had fashioned her whole management style upon feedback given by her early employer: 'He used to let you know how he saw your performance. He held up a mirror to your activities and he highlighted the good and the bad. Seeing myself through his eyes made me change, I recognised the weaknesses and the strengths.'

Mirroring can, of course, be consciously employed to alter someone's feelings about herself, and it is now an established therapeutic technique in clinical circles. The psychologist, in this case, deliberately emulates a client's behaviour so that the client can see from the outside how it looks. The therapy sometimes proceeds with the psychologist introducing new behaviours which can be added to the repertoire and, perhaps, overcome some difficulty troubling the client. Alternatively, it can be deemed sufficient to have shown the client how the difficulty manifests itself in her expression of emotions and attempts at interaction.

The quiet rebel would do well to remember that others are responsive to the mirror that she provides for their behaviour, and consequently she should use this power to shape how they act and change how they feel. She can, by sensibly mirroring their attitudes and incongruous actions, display their inappropriateness. This is of tremendous importance when seeking to overcome role prescriptions which dog relationships at work.

In Chapter 4, some of the roles and interaction rituals which typify relationships at work for the quiet rebel were described. It is important to note that most of these serve to reinforce the move into the no-go emotions. This is most acutely obvious where sexual harassment occurs and the woman rejects the advances made; much of what follows is designed to make the woman feel that she is to blame. She is told that she 'encouraged' the harassment. Often no pretence is made that this 'encouragement' is active, her mere presence in a male environment is taken to be 'encouragement' enough. Simply because she is there, the woman is to blame. It is neither just nor reasonable, but under these circumstances self-blame is alluring. Of course it needs to be resisted at all costs. Once you start to blame yourself for sexual harassment, or any other sort of harassment, you are prey for any creep that comes along.

One way to reassert your blamelessness is by remembering how common sexual harassment actually is. Women of all ages, races, sects, etc, regularly experience it. It is then that you realise that you are not being chased because of your ravishing beauty or those subtle come-hither signals you do not intend to emit. You are being chased purely because it is in the man's interest to do so. So throw self-blame out with the bath water and allot blame to its rightful owner: the social system which dictates the nature of relationships between men and women.

Women who break with tradition in their job choice also suffer guilt to a disproportionate degree. Again it is not surprising. Socialisation practices are designed to make you feel guilty if you fail to do what is expected. In Western cultures, children are taught to have a conscience. Conscience is the keeper of the internalised book of rules: it says what is right and what is wrong according to societal expectations. When its dictates are ignored or contravened, conscience induces guilt. Guilty feelings centre around anxiety, a strangled fear of punishment and doom. Guilt is fundamentally an emotion which hides deep in the psyche. It is the silent watcher's whip which enforces conformity to social expectations. It is interesting that in other cultures guilt is replaced by shame. While guilt is a very individualised experience, shame is a social affair. Shame is imposed by others from outside in a public arena, whereas guilt is imposed by the conscience from within in a private domain. In communities where shaming is a fundamental form of social control, researchers report that people do not experience guilt. They have no internal voice which whispers dire warnings, they are externally controlled. Punishments are not self-inflicted but socially inflicted. Guilt and shame have quite different outcomes. Shame seems to have none of the propensity to generate neurotic disorders which guilt has. The quiet rebel who feels guilty is responding in a predictable way to her circumstances. Guilt is, after all, the guardian of the *status quo*. As a woman, she has been taught to expect to become a good wife and a good mother, and doing a man's job is likely to be seen as antithetical to both of these roles. It is likely that both her husband (if she has one) and her children (if she has any) will reinforce her feelings of guilt. They may not do it with any malicious intent, but they too are subject to social pressures to conform. They too have expectations to fulfil, and part of them is to bring her back into line. They have the job of making her into a good mother and wife. So the children may ask pointed questions such as 'Why aren't you like other mums?' Hubby, who is seen as long-suffering by his male friends because he has to do his fair share of the domestic chores, may wonder aloud why it is that she cannot do the shopping when he is so busy. It takes considerable determination to reject insinuations of guilt of this sort.

It is particularly difficult to evade those from one's children. Children are society's purest propagandists because they have such a dogmatic and categorical grasp of what is correct and what is wrong. Their simplistic understanding of the codes that rule social behaviour permits of no grey areas between black and white. For a child, you are either morally an angel or a devil, and complex qualifying clauses or circumstantial excuses are not permissible. One little girl's response when she first saw a moped typifies this inability to tolerate ambiguity. She wanted to know what the moped was: it had an engine so could be a motor bike, but it also had pedals so it could be a bicycle. Her mother said it was a moped: a motor bike with pedals. The child evinced astonishment, looked sternly at her mother to see whether this was some adult joke, and pronounced, 'Well, it's a very silly motor bike!' It is not difficult to see what she would say about a female electrical engineer.

Children's dogmatism immures them from reason or argument, so they become potent champions of the *status quo*. Of course, that power is exaggerated by the love the quiet rebel has for her children. She does not wish to upset them or make them feel unusual, and since she finds it difficult to use rational argument with them, she is open to the worst excesses of emotional blackmail.

Of course, women who are not married or are without children do not have an easier time. Women who are married and have children might not be good wives and mothers but, at least, they *are* wives and mothers. The woman who remains unmarried and childless has not even entered the race. By still-dominant cultural conceptions, she has to be a failure. She has to feel incomplete. She has to be guilty because she is no real woman.

Val, now in her early thirties, describes how she experiences this pressure. 'I have a career, I have a company which I helped to start and which depends on my drive and knowledge to continue. The business takes most of my waking hours and I have never found a man willing to settle for second place in my life, so I've never married. Until recently, the omission of a husband and/or a child did not bother me. But now I am starting to wonder whether I should take the plunge before it is too late. I have this strange sense of the urgency of my making a decision. Yet I am torn in two directions: I want my career *and* I want a family. It disgusts me that in our time, in our country, this appears to be a virtual impossibility. What is worse is that I know that I will be pitied and envied if I decide to stick solely to my career. I already feel my hackles rise as women with children assume that I should have no opinions about kids which are valid because I have never gone through the pains of childbirth or the hassle of nappy-changing. I already get hints that they think I'm a cold bitch in whom something must have malfunctioned because the old maternal instinct is not on overdrive overwhelming my rationality. I know they think I am letting the side down and believe that I should be guilty about it. I am damned if I will be.'

At work, in a man's job, the unmarried woman is subject to sexual suspicion. After she reaches a certain age, her sexual proclivities become a matter for speculation. Is she more interested in women than in men? Assuming her to be lesbian, or potentially so, solves a lot of problems. It may actually serve as an explanation for her peculiar choice of job. It certainly explains why she should breach their expectations of a good woman. It also, even in our enlightened times, by simply labelling her, serves to deprecate her. Pity the unmarried, childless, heterosexual, middle-aged women who are reproached both for what they are and for what they are not.

Candy is forty; she has never been married, and she is heterosexual. 'Being unmarried and working in a job normally done by a man, surrounded by men daily, does cause difficulties. I used to find that the wives of male co-workers considered me a terrible threat. After several years, when I did not run off with anybody else's husband nor acquire one of my own, I noticed that they seemed to divide into two schools of thought. Some have decided I'm frigid and frightened of sex. The others think I'm gay but hide it well. The latter group watch for me to show any signs of friendliness towards any other woman at work or outside. Snide asides about having seen me at the theatre with my 'friend', and so on, often crop up. I don't know how to stop it, short of having a highly publicised affair with a man. I regard my private life as my own and I am not willing to justify myself to anyone. Nevertheless, I find I get embarrassed, and I think twice before making close women friends. Don't you think that is a terrible shame?'

Women in atypical jobs are especially subject to the no-go emotions of self-doubt, self-blame and guilt. The no-go emotions must be avoided or controlled, because they lead to depression and anxiety. All three break your will to continue, and they are antithetical to the self-assertion and dominance which are so important for success in most jobs. They hem you round and trap you, making you unhappy and making you lose confidence. How can they be controlled?

Controlling the No-Go Emotions

There are four things to remember when you control your no-go emotions:

RULE 1: ALLOCATE BLAME OR GUILT REALISTICALLY

Sometimes things go wrong and it is your fault. We all make

mistakes. But many times things go wrong and it is not your fault. The important thing is to distinguish between the two and only accept responsibility for things falling apart when you truly believe that something you *consciously* did or failed to do precipitated the collapse. That little word 'consciously' is important. There is no point in blaming yourself for things you never intended to do. Blaming yourself for accidents, particularly other people's accidents, is a pernicious mistake. Too often women utter an automatic apology whenever something goes wrong, regardless of who was at fault. The word 'sorry' seems habitually on their lips. It may on the surface seem an unimportant social mannerism that carries no real meaning, but it reflects a state of mind. In becoming realistic about the attachment of blame, a good first step is to exorcise the automatic 'sorry' from your vocabulary.

In order to be discriminating about accepting blame, you need to look carefully at all the evidence. There are three sorts of evidence you might concentrate on: distinctiveness, consistency, and consensus. Look at them in turn. Consensus refers to whether it happens only to you or whether many other people have the same problem. Take the sexual harassment example. If a woman believed she was the only one experiencing the problem, she might conclude she was in some way to blame. If she knows that many other women have exactly the same problem, it becomes clear that she is not uniquely initiating the problem. So, in allotting blame, look for evidence of consensus. Also look for evidence of consistency. Consistency refers to the fact that the problem happens to you over and over again. The more frequently the problem happens to you (especially if it only seems to happen to you), the more likely you are to think that it is your fault. Women who are consistently subject to sexual harassment tend to assume that they are to blame, but only if they believe that other women are not having the same problems. The final sort of evidence is distinctiveness evidence.

This refers to whether the problem is general or very specific. The woman who is harassed only by Tom is likely to think he is responsible; the woman who is harassed by Tom, Dick and Harry is much more likely to think she is herself to blame.

The three sorts of evidence should not be taken in isolation; it is the way they co-vary which allows you to allocate blame. So, for instance, if consensus is low (it only happens to you), consistency is high (it always happens to you), and distinctiveness is low (everybody does it to you), it is about time you accepted the blame. Otherwise, forget it. There are other explanations and you do not need to take the blame.

Examine the information for clues as to who or what is really to blame. Once you have decided who is really to blame—*tell them*. Let them know what you know. If you keep quiet about it, they can carry on blaming you. If you keep quiet about it, you may start to doubt whether you are right. If you keep quiet about it, you never give them a fair chance to explain themselves. If you keep quiet about it, they will not have the information which may form the basis for them changing their ways. Do not keep quiet about it. Tell them.

POWER TALK

What is more, they need to be told in a firm convincing way. Women's patterns of speech are different from those of men on the whole. Research has shown that the forms of speech most used by women are common to all groups of people in our society who are in subordinate positions. Women's speech has therefore been called 'powerless talk'. Powerless talk is perceived as emotional and flowery (replete with unnecessary adjectives and adverbs). It includes more hesitant qualifiers ('maybe', 'perhaps', 'probably') and more hedges ('would I be right in saying?', 'this is true, I think, but there are other opinions'). It uses questioning intonations in statements, so that factual assertions sound like queries and lose their force. It rebounds with tag questions ('this is silly, isn't it?'). Powerless talk has been found to be less persuasive and less attractive. In fact, people using powerless talk are considered less honest and trustworthy. Surprisingly, many women will not believe that they personally use powerless talk. Relatively successful strong women are particularly likely to claim that they do not have such linguistic foibles. It is worthwhile doing a check on your own speech patterns. Listen in on yourself next time you try to persuade someone that you are right and they are wrong. Just count how many times you come up with the qualifiers. It is often surprising.

Women are surprised by their own powerless talk because they are so frequently told that they are verbally dominant. They are told that they have greater fluency and that they talk more than men. There is a whole tradition of proverbs that embody this image of women as having endlessly open mouths (e.g. 'A woman's tongue is the last thing about her that dies'). This contrasts markedly with the evidence of recent years from studies of conversations between men and women. Men talk more than women and are listened to more by both men and women. Women when they talk are more subject to interruptions. Men interrupt women to control the topic of conversation, so that women often have difficulty pursuing a line of discussion in a mixed conversation. Women tend to seek to re-enter a conversation by the use of questions. The problem with this tactic is that questions which do not fire the man's imagination are ignored and those which do simply set him off on another long monologue. Either way, the woman does not achieve an equal partnership in the conversation. Measured in the crudest terms, this inequality is reflected in the sheer length of time each speaks, who chooses the topic for discussion, verbosity, and the number of interruptions. This disparity occurs even when powerful women interact with men of lower status.

Rectifying the imbalance is not merely a matter of women abandoning powerless forms of talk. When women do so, when they drop the hesitancy and portrayal of uncertainty, they are likely to be perceived as rude and ungracious. A woman who adopts power talk is seen as more extroverted, confident and bold, but also as in breach of social expectations. For the quiet rebel, the pay-off in increased assertiveness and persuasiveness is accompanied by a subsidiary increase in unusualness.

It may be difficult to alter one's linguistic style for reasons quite distinct from the social suspicion it engenders. Language is an important symbol of identity, and is a highly visible (or audible) sign of membership of a particular group, class, race, etc. People show through their accent, pronunciation, pause patterns, lexicon, and so on where and what they come from. The way we speak symbolises a lot about who we are. It is consequently difficult to give up speech styles, because that means losing part of our self-expression. Speech styles are maintained often long after the person moves into new social worlds. The man who has lived in an urban setting for years but maintains his rural accent and dialect is unconsciously emphasising an important aspect of his identity. The successful female executive who eschews power talk is reaffirming her femininity. People will tenaciously adhere to what are sometimes highly stigmatised forms of speech, because they satisfy identity needs.

When allocating blame, the quiet rebel has to overcome the tendency to use powerless talk. She has to lodge the blame where it should really lie. She will be ignored if she uses powerless talk, and will find herself heaped with a double blame: for the original error, and for the failed attempt at shifting it to someone else. She needs to be clear and firm and to recognise that the identity reflected in powerless talk is only leading her into trouble. If she uses power talk she may not be thought genteel or civil, but she will be thought effective. They may not like what she has to tell them, but the way that she tells them will communicate volumes about her ability and determination.

RULE 2: BEWARE THE STANDARD TRAPS

Watch out for the standard interaction rituals described in Chapter 4, which are structured to leave you feeling guilty or doubtful. Recognise that the ritual is designed to insult you. Other people are using the ritual to treat you like a punchbag and claim that you like hanging from the ceiling and swinging about after every blow.

In dealing with these traps, all you have to do is remember that the ritual cannot be enacted to its completion unless you play your role. If you throw a spanner in the works by failing to supply the stock responses which are expected of you, the thing breaks down before they have a chance to reach the punchline and hit you with the full dose of guilt and doubt. Ways of cutting short the routine are outlined in the self-exercises in Chapter 8.

Above all, remember that the set piece ritual interchange is meaningless. It should never be taken seriously as a comment on your personal abilities or responsibilities. It should never be taken at face value. The trick is to analyse it for the motives which underlie it. You should make a habit of disrupting any rituals which irritate you or do not act to your advantage.

RULE 3: HOLD TO YOUR OWN STANDARDS OF SUCCESS

This is a really difficult rule to follow. It means that you set your own criteria for success and failure and allot blame to yourself only when you fail according to those criteria. It is difficult, because everyone else wants to set criteria for us. Often they want us to accept jobs, roles, and expectations which are antithetical to our own wishes. When we fail to succeed in these tasks that we never wanted to do, they call us failures.

Failure in something where you never wanted success is not really failure. Only when you fail in relation to your self-imposed goals should you accept blame and maybe begin to doubt yourself.

To do this you need continually to keep in mind who is setting the goals and what you personally wish to achieve. When someone comes along with claims that you have failed on a goal that you never sought to achieve, tell them firmly it was not your objective and you have no reason to believe, therefore, that you have failed.

People will set you unrealistic objectives if you let them. Do not let them.

It is equally important to seek to get other people to recognise that the objectives you have set for yourself are valid and worth attaining. Otherwise you will be continually receiving negative feedback from them. Since mirroring is so strong a tendency, you may start to feel negative about yourself if you allow them to continue viewing your activities in a negative way. Persuading them that you are right in the goals you have chosen can elicit vital support. Once they start seeing the value of the targets you seek, you will mirror their esteem and grow in confidence and determination.

RULE 4: QUERY THE MOTIVES OF ANYONE WHO SUGGESTS YOU DOUBT YOURSELF

Always ask a simple question when someone suggests that you are doing the wrong thing: what do they get out of it? Unless you believe that their motives are crystal clear and totally pure, it is best to ignore them.

A certain amount of self-doubt can be adaptive. It can be useful in stopping you over-reaching yourself. But mostly it is useless and immobilises you. Over-confidence is more likely to succeed than doubt, and if you doubt yourself, others will doubt you. It is an example of the mirroring process in reverse. Err on the side of confidence, and other people will have confidence in you.

These four rules are central to the control of the no-go emotions, but it is not easy to abide by the rules. In the next chapter some techniques for strengthening the psychological muscles that hold you to the rules are described.

Further Reading

Spender, D., *Man Made Language*. London: Routledge and Kegan Paul, 1980.

Giles, H. and St. Clair, R. (eds), *Language and Social Psychology*. Oxford: Blackwell, 1979.

Bouchard Ryan, E. and Giles, H. (eds), *Attitudes towards Language Variation*. London: Arnold, 1982.

Hewstone, M. (ed.), *Attribution Theory: Social and Functional Aspects*. Oxford: Blackwell, 1983.

Chapter Seven
SELF-EXERCISES

The self-concept, that image we harbour of our own attributes and value, is like a living organism: it needs sustenance to survive. It needs to be fed a diet of information, which confirms it, and respect, which enhances it. Like a plant deprived of light or water, the self-concept refused appropriate social support will shrivel into dormancy or decay. Since the quiet rebel stands outside the system of social expectations in vital ways, she is denied the standard scaffolding of the self-concept. She has to fight for acceptance for her self. Problems encountered in relationships in the workplace or subsequently at home are so traumatic often because they strike at the very heart of the self-concept. They reflect a refusal to acknowledge her for what she believes herself to be or, if they concede her self-definition to be accurate, they deplore it. Sometimes these rejections lead to changes in the self-concept which are valuable, shifting the quiet rebel to greater realism or responsiveness. Often they are simply destructive, tearing down the façade of the self without reconstruction. The quiet rebel has to learn how to repulse such destructive onslaughts, and there are a number of tactics that can be used to do so. They focus upon ways of viewing one's self and ways of dealing with other people.

Self-Maintenance

Women who have a lot to do (running a home, a family, and a job) tend to neglect self-maintenance. They have so little time for anything other than routine tasks or imperative reactions to crises, that they skimp on the energy they devote to their self. Self-maintenance entails more than just the physical upkeep of the body, though physical fitness and turnout are important — it is comforting to feel in peak form, to dress well and to make the most of good looks. It also involves setting time aside for reflection and examination of feelings and thoughts. Without such time-outs for self-examination, it is possible to lose contact with the world of the emotions. Feelings, whether positive or negative, are shunned; if admitted, no time is given over to understanding their origin and their consequences. Women find themselves too busy to recognise when they are happy and the reasons for it, or what makes them fearful and its outcomes. The emotions of the day rush by without acknowledgement like street lamps beside the passage of the speeding car, and it becomes difficult to know whether the emotions other people would ascribe to you are accurate reflections of the way you feel. When others attribute self-blame, guilt and self-doubt, there is no pre-existent standard to compare them against.

Some women simply get into the habit of squeezing emotion-ality out of their schedule. It is not that the emotions actually go away, but they are just not paid any attention. Not having to confront your own feelings, especially negative ones like fear, anxiety, or sadness, has its own rewards: you carry on functioning within the illusion of emotional ease. But the respite is, in truth, temporary. Emotions exist to shape thought and action; ignore them, and they grow until they succeed in their original purpose of changing what you think and do, because they are too big to be ignored. Emotions allowed to fester in the dark can ultimately have explosive impacts upon behaviour. For instance, the quiet rebel will often be angered by some event at work; if the anger is suppressed, it will tend to subterranean expansion and will erupt unexpectedly in response to a trivial occurrence and out of all proportion to the immediate problem. Losing track of feelings, or denial of them, can consequently be hazardous.

Self-maintenance is designed to prevent this happening. It means setting aside a regular time for reflection on how you have been feeling and why. Self-maintenance can be combined with other routine chores as long as they are undemanding, and it need not take long. Ten minutes in the bath at the end of the day, or while washing the dishes or re-potting the geraniums, is all it takes. The process is most effective if done systematically. First, identify the day's major happenings; second, specify what emotions they evoked in you and the other people involved; third, describe to yourself how you expressed or repressed your emotion on each occasion; and finally, decide whether what you did made you feel better or worse. Such time devoted to self-analysis is the precursor of decisions about what changes need to be wrought in order to bring life more under your control.

Women vary in how they conduct their self-analysis. Jo, a recently promoted Principal Lecturer at a College of Education, used to find that so many new things happened to her each day that it was impossible to sleep at night. The events of the day and the confusions she felt simply carried on whirring around her head. She realised lack of sleep only compounded the pressure she felt during the day, and her answer has been to clear her mind by spending twenty minutes or so before bed writing a work diary in which she records the major events and emotions. It is a highly selective diary, consisting only of events which have troubled or moved her. It crystallises her thoughts and allows her to plan what needs to happen next, and she finds that it has enabled her to stop thinking about work before she goes to bed and so her sleep is better. She argues that the period of writing the diary acts like a filing system: information and emotions are packed away with notes for further action. She believes that once she is more used to the job, the need actually to write everything down will pass, and she will be able to do the same thing in thought, but for the time being the written record is essential to her sweet dreams.

So far, self-maintenance has been treated as an isolated activity, but it does not have to be. Most people use their friends and intimates in the process of self-maintenance; they are employed as sounding boards for self-description and evaluation. In fact, achieving satisfying intimacy depends upon carefully timed *self-disclosure*. At the start of a relationship, disclosures have to be only trivial and commonplace, socially-desirable self-portraits. Disclosures which go too deep, too fast, will frighten the potential friend. It is only after a gradual strip-tease, in which successive layers of the self are bared, that the bond will be established firmly enough for genuine attempts at self-exploration to be feasible.

Self-disclosures, once the bond is established, can be about one's innermost fears, hopes and disappointments. One woman pointed out: 'I need to tell somebody about how frustrated I get at work. I watch myself being passed over for promotion and retraining in favour of men who "need to be brought on so that their future career is assured" and I could explode. I know that such displays of emotion at work would only count against me, so I bottle it up and let loose at home. My flatmate has to have patience. He listens to all my anger and disappointment. It is important that he really listens; it is not just talk but a real sharing of feelings. He tells me all his frustrations in return. It took time for me to come to trust him with my secret feelings, but now I don't know what I would do without him.'

Friendless people often fail to understand the dynamics of self-disclosure. They want a confidant so desperately that they reveal too much, too soon, and lose their chance. They also fail to understand that the process is two-way: self-disclosure has to be mutual to be optimally effective, so it is necessary to listen as well as talk.

As one woman said: 'Some people in big cities are so lonely that they'd tell the story of their lives on the Clapham omnibus. But it means nothing. You might as well be a brick wall for all they care. It is not sharing feelings. For it to be meaningful, it has to be mutual.'

As long as self-disclosure is well-timed and pursued mutually, it can be a valuable tool of self-maintenance. It enables the woman to check whether someone else, whom she trusts, interprets events in the same way she does. It validates or extends her own understandings, and may offer a safe arena in which to express emotions that cannot be let loose elsewhere without enormous disruption. Within the relationship she can get rid of anger, fear or hate without reprisals. From it, she can seek appraisals of her coping strategies and probably learn of new ones.

Many quiet rebels cut themselves off from this sort of support relationship. The reasons for doing so are varied: lack of time to see friends, the belief that no one else can possibly understand their unique problems, the fear that such a need reflects weakness, and so on. Whatever the reason, it is a mistake.

The woman who practises self-maintenance and uses self-disclosure stands a much better chance of resisting the pressures which collude to ravage her self-image and self-esteem.

Negativism

Negativism is another good ploy to have available in need. It is the state of mind one is in when one feels a desire, or a compulsion, to act *against* the requirements or pressures from some external source. There are lots of familiar expressions to describe negativism: 'bloody-mindedness', 'cussedness', 'trouble-seeking', 'cantankerousness', and so on. Negativism is deliberately saying 'no'. Some psychologists have argued that we come to know who and what we are by saying 'no' to what we are not. Knowing is no-ing, to put it tritely. They even go so far as to suggest that the Bible tells that man became Man only through disobedience — to God that is, as opposed to Eve, whom he agreed with at the time.

Less speculatively, it is known that negativism characterises all of the great life transitions. It is typical of children between the ages of 1½ and 3½ years. Through disobedience they demonstrate a growing psychological independence that matches their increasing physical independence. Only through negativism can a child develop the concept of her own will power. It makes its next great appearance during adolescence, when the young person is seeking sexual and social independence and when she is acquiring new abstract thinking capacities which allow her to understand more of what it is possible to refuse. Negativism is also notable in old age. Then the loss of autonomy which physical decline imports generates renewed negativism that represents a hedge against despair and against the debilitation of institutionalisation.

Though most visible in these periods of life crisis, negativism is a perpetual possibility and an important foundation for the self-concept. A person requires a self-concept which is distinctive, continuous, and independent. Distinctiveness can only be achieved by being willing to reject some of the standard expectations and orthodoxies in the interests of creativity; such rejection is fundamentally negativism. Continuity requires the ability to refuse to change despite attempts to impose change; such refusal is basically negativism. Independence is founded on resistance to influence; such resistance is derived from negativism. Negativism is useful in strengthening all three aspects of the self-concept.

Negativism, like all powerful processes, is two-edged, and can have detrimental effects if it gets out of hand. This normally happens in three ways. Firstly, continuity can clash with distinctiveness needs, and negativism in the interests of one can attack the other aspect of the self-concept. For instance, the quiet rebel, in the interests of continuity of self-image, might refuse to join a group, a club or a society which would have offered her tremendous kudos and distinctiveness. Of course, it can happen the other way round, where she joins the group and gains distinctiveness but loses continuity, her self-concept being irreparably changed by the new membership. This sort of problem with negativism is normally simple to solve because the individual can say whether continuity or distinctiveness is more important to her under the circumstances. As long as she can then control her negativism, things are fine, but in some cases, control evaporates and gives rise to the second type of problem. Some people suffer from *hypernegativism*. Their rejections, resistance and refusals are too generalised and too vicious; they cannot draw the line between productive and counterproductive negativism. Psychopaths are commonly supposed to be characterised by this tendency. The third dysfunction is known as *self-negativism*. It tends to occur when the person feels it is impossible to resist the real source of pressure and redirects the anger or whatever emotion is generated against herself. Self-negativism is thus reflected in masochism, ascetism, self-sacrifice, and self-damage ranging from nail-biting to suicide.

Despite its darker connotations, negativism is a valuable tool. The quiet rebel is hemmed in by pressures to conform; often they are actually demanding change in mutually exclusive directions. She has to be able to say 'no' to some or else she will be torn apart. Conforming to domestic requirements may mean that conforming to job demands is impossible, or vice versa; something has to give and, hopefully, it will not be the psychological well-being of the woman involved.

For the quiet rebel with little experience of negativism, practice is a good idea. Choose in advance a situation which you would like to resist, work out what standard interaction rituals are involved and when you should issue your refusal, practise in your mind what you will say, and say it on the very next opportunity. It is normal to feel anxious before such an act of negativism, but the reward follows after with an enormous sense of relief often ensuing. It is probably best to start with small, relatively insignificant acts of negativism to prove to yourself that it is possible. Choose a situation where a refusal is possible but where you would not normally think to do so. For instance, when asked to continue to do a job that costs you little effort but which you had thought to pass on quicker and where you could legitimately refuse, do so. The point about this sort of negativism is that it builds your confidence in the very possibility of being successful in refusing and also serves to alert colleagues that you will not always respond with immediate compliance. They then realise that they may have to spend longer convincing you that their ideas are good or worth your time. By being discriminating in your responses, you make your opinion count more because it is no longer a foregone conclusion.

The key message is: use negativism, not universally, but with forethought and discriminatingly.

Examples of the effective use of negativism can be drawn from various contexts. For instance, there are many ways of saying 'no'. One woman, a middle manager in a large corporation, describes how she now regularly uses the 'deflection tactic': 'At meetings where jobs are being doled out, I make a point of accepting a difficult task that interests me whenever I can and preferably early in the meeting. I then have a prime justification for refusing others, and when asked to do trivial or less interesting things, I suggest that a colleague, preferably one not present, is far better suited to that job than I. It serves a number of functions. Not least, it offers me the chance of seeming busier and more knowledgeable than colleagues.' Another uses the 'stonewall tactic'. She says: 'I found that being the only woman director of the company meant that the others seemed to think I would collapse under pressure if I disagreed with a proposed course of action. At first I adopted a sort of democratic stance. If everyone else voted against me, I gave in. Now, though, I carry on arguing for my standpoint. Sometimes I do it even if I've been persuaded. I find that my awkwardness means that I am kept better informed of what is happening because they try to persuade me in private before a meeting instead of in public.' This argumentative approach takes courage but is actually effective. There is a whole body of social psychological evidence to show that if you talk more in a decision-making group — even if you talk rubbish — you are regarded by the participants as more important and powerful. Women who acquiesce in silence lose not only their right to influence a decision but also their image as a leader.

Stress

The last decade has seen the rise of 'stress' as a major means of explaining a vast array of physical illnesses and psychological collapse. It has taken the place of evil spirits and moral turpitude as the root of all the world's ills. Stress is used as a catch-all term to connote anything and everything that can do harm. Stress is a disease of a post-industrial society that has done away with witch-doctors and most of its priests but which still needs an easy explanation of its inexplicable ailments. What causes stress? Anything can be stressful; it all depends on how you look at it. What can stress cause? It can cause anything; it is the universal mediator.

The stress concept only really becomes useful when it is tied down to specific sorts of problem and types of response. In the workplace there are six major sources of stress, and it can be argued that the quiet rebel is liable to be susceptible to them all.

1. *Job requirements* are often stressful: working to tight deadlines, travelling long distances, putting in long hours, tackling demanding tasks, act as stressors. All are tied to higher risks of coronary heart disease, escapist drinking, lowered self-esteem, and higher levels of absenteeism.

2. *Organisation roles* which are either ambiguous or fraught with conflict are stressful. Role ambiguity occurs where the person is uncertain as to what is expected as part of the job. It is most frequent where areas of responsibility are not clearly defined or rules for task allocation are unspecified. Role conflict occurs when goals are clearly articulated but where several mutually exclusive ones are included: the person is expected to be in two places at once; to take two quite different attitudes to subordinates; to complete two tasks simultaneously. Both ambiguity and conflict lead to psychological and physiological distress: depression and apathy, and higher prevalence of coronary-heart-disease risk factors (like higher blood pressure, pulse rate and serum cholesterol levels). Since the unusual presence of the quiet rebel is likely to make her a prime target for role ambiguity and conflict, these findings are of considerable concern.

3. *Poor relationships* with superiors or subordinates is another powerful source of stress.

4. *Career prospects* are tied to stress perception: job insecurity and thwarted promotion heighten stress.

5. *Home-work demands* which are in conflict to the extent that neither can be adequately satisfied generate stress.

6. *Organisational networks* at work which deny the person access to decision-making cause higher physiological and mental

risks, lower productivity and encourage resignation.

While all quiet rebels may face fundamentally similar patterns of stress at work, and while these may be mirrored at home, their responses will differ greatly. Responses depend on personality and the coping resources that are available.

Personality and Stress

Not everyone faced with a source of stress succumbs to physical or psychological breakdown. Over the last twenty years, psychologists have built up a picture of the personality most prone to stress reactions. These individuals have been referred to as 'coronary-prone behaviour pattern Type As'.

Type A personalities are characterised by extreme competitiveness, striving for achievement, aggressiveness, haste, impatience, restlessness, hyper-alertness, explosiveness of speech, tenseness of facial musculature, feelings of being under pressure of time, and challenge of responsibility. Typically, they are so deeply involved in their work that other areas of life are neglected and devalued.

Numerous studies have shown that Type A people, as opposed to Type Bs who lack these characteristics, succumb to the most profound physical and psychological effects of stress. One study reported that by the time they are in their forties, Type A men are over six times more likely to have suffered heart problems, particularly acute myocardial infarction and angina pectoris, and these are more likely to be recurrent and fatal. It is interesting that personality type seems more important than type of work. The same pattern of results is found among Trappist and Benedictine monks. The point is, however, that personality type predisposes to negative, non-adaptive responses to stress: where stress is extreme, in high pressure jobs, the dangers of being a Type A are magnified.

This is one of those areas where the sexist bias of psychology is evident. The studies of the relation of women's personality to stress are few. So direct evidence is lacking. However, there seems no reason to suppose *a priori* a sex difference in this matter. Type A women may be less numerous, but no less at risk.

For the quiet rebel who recognises in herself the typical Type A personality, there is still room for self-preservation strategies. Personality does not fixedly predetermine responses to stress, it interacts with a number of other factors in shaping them. Central amongst these are the coping strategies and resources available to the individual.

Habitual Coping Strategies

During the course of their lives people evolve preferred methods of coping with stress. These become habitual, being applied indiscriminately whenever stress arises, and can become maladaptive. One such is denial: the distressing reality is simply denied. It is a game in which you pretend that the thing (or person) which upsets you is not really there. In fact, denial can be a complex game with a series of stages. First, the facts are denied, then their relevance, then their urgency, then your responsibility to act, then the way you feel and, finally, the importance of how you feel. The process is seen in its fiercest form where illness is concerned. People refuse to accept that they see the symptoms, then, once they are acknowledged, reject their significance. If they recognised their relevance, they often will not realise the urgency or importance of action. Having acted, they still resist admitting how they feel or what their feelings mean. The danger of denial is clearest when it results in inactivity where remedial action taken early might be the difference between recovery and death. The benefits of denial are evident where people told that they have a terminal illness will not passively collude with the diagnosis but fight on. The situations where the quiet rebel might employ denial may not be quite so dramatic, but they share similar dangers and pay-offs. The quiet rebel who denies, even to herself, that she is being passed over for promotion, may lose the opportunity to change what is happening. The quiet rebel who knows that she has been passed over but who denies that it is important, may survive the blow better than most. It really all comes down to a matter of what and when you deny.

Habitual coping strategies seem to change with age. As a rule, people move from aggressive to more passive coping strategies. However, it is worth pointing out that women seem to become more aggressive in their strategies during middle age, when men show a marked shift to passivity. This is probably no accident: men's passivity gives women greater room for aggression and vice versa. The changes with age are most likely to arise because the sources of stress alter and resources for coping broaden as people grow older. Stress shifts from financial and interpersonal concerns to physical worries.

Habitual coping strategies are further constrained by personal belief systems and by environmental context. Beliefs and systems of values will predispose their adherents to certain strategies rather than others. For instance, some people would eschew social support in times of stress because they hate the idea of dependency; others would avoid a doctor because of religious principles; and more would retreat from a psychiatrist because of the stereotype held of mental illness.

Environmental factors influence coping strategies simply and directly through social institutions and laws which control the provision of services and limit personal freedom. A facile example might be the case of the woman who needed money but who was prevented from stealing it not by moral principle but by the strong arm of the law. A less facile example might be the case of the woman seeking release from a lingering fatal illness for whom euthanasia would be a personal choice, but who is refused it by society.

The quiet rebel facing stress needs to examine how far her coping strategies are merely thoughtless habits, and to evaluate their efficacy and how far it is actually feasible to change them, given her beliefs and society's restraints.

Focus for Coping

Coping strategies can focus upon the problem causing stress or upon the emotions created by stress. Problem-focused coping is targeted at changing the situation such that stress is eradicated. It can mean changing the social or physical environment or, indeed, changing oneself (learning new skills, modifying beliefs, and so on). Emotion-focused coping strategies do not change the objective reality, they merely change the psychological meaning or importance of that reality. Emotion-focused strategies are designed to revise the feelings aroused by the stress.

Sometimes the same stressful situation can evoke either problem-focused or emotion-focused coping strategies; it will depend upon the way the individual woman is used to coping with stress. For instance, a woman executive might be faced with the introduction into offices that she manages of new information-processing machines. This would be stressful if she did not understand the new technology involved and perhaps felt that she was losing touch with new developments in her industry. There are at least two ways of dealing with the stress experienced. The first is problem-focused: she could eliminate the source of stress by ensuring that she acquired an understanding of the new systems before their introduction by going on a course or getting some form of instruction in their structure and functions. The second is emotion-focused: she could take steps to control her feelings of anxiety about the new developments without actually gaining any new understanding of them. The first coping strategy is designed to remove the source of the stress (her ignorance); the second is aimed at allowing her to tolerate the discomfort initiated by that problem. Emotion-focused and problem-focused strategies can be used in unison but do not necessarily help each other. They can hinder each other, especially where the reconstrual of reality demanded by the emotion-focused approach means that the objective situation is no longer adequately understood. Problem-solving is then founded upon misconceptions of the facts and can go seriously awry. For this reason, most methods developed by psychologists for dealing with stress either concentrate on the problem or on the emotions rather than attempting to synthesise or integrate those approaches.

Stress Management

The stress management techniques evolved by psychologists vary in the extent to which they are truly amenable to usage by the individual without assistance. Most of them require direct communication between the psychologist and the client. They are tailored to the needs of the individual and dependent upon interaction with the counsellor. However, recently there has been an increase in self-help manuals designed to guide people through stress. These provide general rules or principles about how stress may be managed, and in most cases the principles are derived from methods used in clinical practice which have proven successful. The manuals allow people to become their own psychologist, but unfortunately few have been tested for the method's efficacy when used in this do-it-yourself way. It is possible that, when removed from close supervision and control, the methods lose their power. It is even more likely that when boiled down to general principles and communalities they lose their individual relevance. Consequently, do-it-yourself guides to coping with stress have to be used with some caution. They are not miracle cures and they need to be used with sensitivity of interpretation. The user has to ensure that they are tailored to her particular needs and has to choose from amongst the battery available the ones which best suit her. With that word of warning, those below are offered for consideration and trial.

SYSTEMATIC DESENSITISATION

This method is essentially emotion-focused. It is designed to reduce the anxiety experienced in relation to a particular stress situation by allowing the person to face it while relaxed. The steps in the procedure are as follows: locate the source of anxiety, isolate it from its context, and allow yourself to break it down into its constituent parts; then try to deal with it bit by bit in circumstances which facilitate calmness and confidence. The approach is known as systematic desensitisation because it is a gradual process of becoming less acutely responsive to a situation: it unhooks the anxiety response from the problem. It is premised on the notion that anxiety is a learned response which can be unlearned.

In practice, desensitisation involves achieving relaxation and then initially only thinking about the problem, breaking off if anxiety is aroused. Once you can think about it without anxiety, you progress to practising what you might do in the situation, again stopping the moment anxiety destroys the calmness. Ultimately, the object is to be able to face the problem in reality without the automatic anxiety response because the relaxation you have learnt to associate with it inhibits other emotions.

The technique is a cornerstone of behaviour modification therapies and is thought to work well where problems can be clearly identified and brought into the relaxing domain for control. For instance, it is used to control phobias. Fear of heights, terror of public speaking, horror of snakes, all can be controlled using desensitisation. The quiet rebel suffering anxiety in easily specified contexts might consider trying a little do-it-yourself desensitisation. An example would be where she finds herself very anxious when she has to speak in a meeting where she is the only woman. Her anxiety is disabling and she would like to control it. The first step would be to sit quietly alone and calm herself; after a while, once completely relaxed, she might try to remember an occasion in a meeting where she was unable to talk. She has to try to face the situation in her imagination without allowing anxiety to build and while keeping her calmness steady. Once she can think of such situations without the slightest rumble of butterflies in the stomach, then she can go on to try it in the real thing. Again, relaxation has to be achieved first (and can be aided by physical means like deep breathing) and maintained. The initial trials might involve only brief interjections into the discussion with withdrawal as soon as anxiety sets in. The object would be to build up the amount of time spent speaking while controlling growth of anxiety. The method will only work if the stages are graduated and planned in advance. Success at each stage generates self-confidence and facilitates further successes later.

Desensitisation can be supplemented by a régime of self-reinforcement. It has long been known that behaviours which are rewarded increase in frequency, while those punished decline. Self-reinforcement entails rewarding oneself for actions and feelings which you wish to happen more often. In the above example, every time she makes a successful contribution to a discussion in a meeting, the quiet rebel might reward herself. The nature of the reward is a matter of personal taste; they range from a new book to a holiday break, from learning a new sport (skydiving, for instance) to a decent bottle of claret, from a quiet evening at home for two to a furious night on the town. It is, however, preferable if they are rewards you can afford.

STRESS INOCULATION

Stress inoculation is currently extensively used in the training of various occupational groups (like the police and the armed services) who have to cope with stressful situations as a normal part of their job. Stress inoculation has three phases: education, rehearsal, and application. During the education phase people are taught how they are likely to feel in a particular stressful situation and why. For instance, the police might be taught about the racial prejudice they are possibly going to feel during a race riot. They will be taught of the hatred, rage and loss of control which can ensue. In a way this is not telling them something new; they know that this is what happens, but the structured discussion of it makes them freshly aware of it. Rehearsal takes the form of role play where they are asked to try out alternative reactions to the situation: rage is replaced by compassion, icy unemotionality, fear, pity, authoritarianism, or whatever. The most effective reaction is then practised, and rehearsed so often that it becomes second nature. Application is the performance for real on the street in the riot. By that stage, they know what to expect and how they should behave, even if they have never seen a live riot before.

The quiet rebel can use the same route to immunity from her own emotions. Stress inoculation works like any other inoculation: it introduces the problem into your system in minute quantities so that you can build up resistance (cognitive and emotional antibodies) to it before you have to encounter the real infection. The quiet rebel tackling sexual harassment could profit from this type of stress inoculation. It is the ideal way to overcome feelings of self-blame or confusion. The rehearsal phase allows the evolution of responses which disrupt interaction rituals that guard the men practising sexual harassment.

Suzy, a very successful astronomer in her early thirties, with a steady boyfriend and a randy boss, used stress inoculation when facing sexual harassment. She commented: 'My problem was that I believed that the harassment was my fault. Almost accidentally I revealed what was happening—you know, the suggestions and the continual sly groping—to a friend; she "educated" me about the incidence of harassment and suggested the stress inoculation method. I thought that I had nothing to lose, so I worked out when he made most of his approaches and the normal pattern they took, and then I worked out how I normally reacted. I would get flushed, flustered, and basically run away. I think this was largely because the last thing I wanted to do was alienate him, since my future career depended on him: I work in a small, close-knit community and any bad publicity travels fast. So I practised how I might respond without offending him but while making sure that my message got through. Not easy. My tactic in the end was to introduce Nigel, my boyfriend, into the conversation every time he tried it and make sure that I did not run away. The spontaneous flight response I had been using had been destroying my confidence in other areas at work, and I knew I had to prove to myself as well as him that I could take it without withdrawal.' Suzy also pointed out that she found the process of analysing the problem rationally and without panic vitally important in restoring her confidence and retrieving her sense of proportion.

BIOFEEDBACK

Besides being able to learn how to control their emotions, people can learn mastery over their physiological responses. Until recently, it was believed by scientists that people had no voluntary control over their autonomic nervous system (the system which is tied to the so-called involuntary bodily processes like pulse rate, blood pressure, pupil dilation, etc.). Yet it is now known that, given the right information, people can alter these processes, and most people have been shown to be able to exert very specific control over such bodily functions. A person can lower the blood pressure in a single finger, while leaving the other three on that hand at standard pressure. Children have been taught to defend against epileptic seizure by blanketing electrical emissions from certain parts of their brains. The key to such control lies in feedback: to affect the system, people need to know how it is varying according to their efforts. Consequently, they are normally wired up to a machine which can monitor changes and passes on information to them. According to the original method, people could be rewarded for effecting a change and this would facilitate future control. However, it was soon discovered that people find the fact that they have control rewarding in itself. The intrinsic reward makes extrinsic rewards for adults unnecessary.

Because of the need for machinery to monitor processes and give biofeedback, the use of such control methods might seem impractical for the quiet rebel; however, this is not altogether true for two reasons. Firstly, once control is achieved under conditions where biofeedback is available, it can be maintained elsewhere even when feedback is not given. Secondly, questions have arisen about the real importance of the feedback itself and how the physiological processes map onto psychological ones. For instance, one biofeedback technique used with headache-sufferers is to get them to relax the major forehead muscle; the reduction in tension is then supposed to waft away the headache. However, recent tests have shown that even if they are given fallacious feedback on the extent of relaxation achieved, as long as they believe the forehead muscle has relaxed the headache disappears. Thus the headache goes even when the tension is as great as ever. This implies that merely the illusion of control of physiological processes is sufficient to effect psychological changes, and means that accuracy in biofeedback, although necessary for physiological change, is not required for psychological change. Admittedly, this may be relevant in only a small proportion of those cases where biofeedback is employed, but it is worth considering.

The quiet rebel wishing to use biofeedback techniques can therefore acquire the skill with the aid of a trainer who has the appropriate monitoring equipment, and can expect to use the control skill later without direct feedback. The range of stress problems biofeedback might help is broader than it might at first appear. Many types of stress will generate harmful physiological changes (increased pulse rate, blood pressure, etc.). Having the power to halt these damaging changes, regardless of how they are initiated, is valuable. Ironically, even believing that you have such power, when you do not, may have psychological advantages in reducing anxiety, fear, and so on that themselves can cause psychosomatic problems like ulcers, asthma, or headaches.

Cynthia employed biofeedback effectively: 'I have to fight every inch of the way to get what I want done. The men working for me in the paper mill I manage have never had a female boss before and want me to prove myself continually. I found that the continual conflict led to me getting very tense during any disagreement. I started to have a really short temper and found myself listening to my own heartbeat pounding in my ears as for the hundredth time in the day I had to vindicate my standpoint. I could feel my system tense and go into overdrive. I knew this was a recipe for failure with the workforce and a short life. So I decided to learn how to control the physical response I had to conflict. I learnt consciously to lower my pulse rate using equipment which gave me information about what I was achieving. It was remarkably successful. Now I can decide to calm my system down when it shows signs of going into overdrive. I also practise relaxation on a daily basis: often only fifteen minutes at lunchtime. I find it tones me up for the rest of the day.'

Though less hedged around with technological hardware, more traditional techniques of communing with one's own body can function like biofeedback. Meditation, practised under direction, can permit the individual to achieve an awareness and, thereby, control of bodily processes. Meditation may take a long time to perfect as a tool of body maintenance. Biofeedback short-cuts the rigours of years of practice. Unfortunately, it also cuts out the beneficial side-effects of meditation: relaxation, time for reflection alone, silence amidst business, and the more suspect mythical-religious baggage most meditational techniques carry.

COGNITIVE APPROACHES

The cognitive approaches are problem-focused coping strategies. They assume that by changing the way a person thinks about a problem that is stressful, its power to induce stress can be conquered and the problem itself becomes more tractable. They are designed not simply to teach the person how to live with the problem with minimum distress, but how to effect changes which make it go away. The cognitive approach relies on coming to understand the problem and thereby coming to know how it might be eradicated. Sometimes understanding rests on ridding yourself of faulty assumptions or prejudices. Often it requires the development of new skills.

An example of the cognitive approach comes from training programmes designed to help those who are having trouble *handling difficult people*, a common source of stress in the work setting, particularly for the quiet rebel. The method has six general steps: assess the situation; avoid wishing (unrealistically) that such people would change or simply go away; distance oneself from the troubling behaviour in order to see it properly and even empathise with it; formulate a coping strategy which could change the unproductive pattern of interaction; implement the plan by first practising how to act or role-playing it with a friend and then choosing an appropriate time for confrontation; monitor what is done to assess why it might not be working and perhaps, if all else fails, work out the possibilities for avoiding that person.

People are disagreeable in different ways, and part of the cognitive approach is to suggest which strategies might work best with each type of disagreeableness. For indecisive people, it is suggested that they should be helped to express their concerns and conflicts, be provided with support, and that choice alternatives offered them should be strictly limited to facilitate decisiveness. For hostile and aggressive people, the strategy is to stand up to them without being drawn into an open fight, the accent being upon controlling your own anger to prevent them dictating how the confrontation proceeds; once tempers are ignited, the naturally aggressive person has a large advantage. For the know-it-all, the advice is to restrict yourself to making factual not dogmatic statements; devolving into a war of unfounded assertions is quite pointless, and it may even pay to accept a subordinate role if this means that what has to be done is accomplished. For the complainer, a good dose of cold water is recommended: complaints should be paid no attention or should be discouraged with graduated punishments; where complaints are replaced by constructive suggestions or helpful comments, the person should be rewarded. Shaping of behaviour with rewards and punishments can work with unresponsive, negativistic and even overagreeable people, too.

Sometimes the use of what are called *self-statements* can be helpful in overcoming the faulty premises which can misdirect thoughts and feelings in a stressful situation. Self-statements are simple descriptions which are designed to block the encroachment of unproductive habits. They act as a mnemonic in times of stress to prevent the person losing track of what is true amid the pressures surrounding her. Useful self-statements for the quiet rebel might include: 'I'm not any less of a woman because I do men's work'; 'I am not always to blame'; 'What I have to say is important'; 'I have competence and confidence'; 'Success is good for me', and so on. Self-statements can be used like a mantra to clear the mind of all else, to eradicate its doubt and shield it from outside messages. They can be picked up as a silent refrain by the inner voice, lullabies that herald the ability to sleep at night. The self-statement can be used to gag all those other doubting voices which cause insomnia.

Self-statements are really only one way of introducing changes in beliefs or attitudes which may be required by the cognitive approach. Any of the attitude change methods discussed in Chapter 8 can be used in addition. The means of bringing about change is not important, as long as the change permits the problem to be tackled more efficiently. The trick lies in identifying which attitudes are causing the difficulty. In some instances they may be obvious. Take the example of the quiet rebel required to keep the day-to-day accounts of her division of the firm as a peripheral part of her job, who finds it an impossible task. Her incompetence in this area is a source of public humiliation and cannot be ignored. It is not just a matter of coping with the anxiety aroused, she has to solve the problem and master the accounts. At the root of the problem may be the fact that she believes book-keeping to require mathematical abilities she has never possessed and which she consequently denigrates and avoids. Her beliefs about her skills and her attitudes to her skills block any attempt to solve her problem. Her attitudes may even have the power to prevent her acquiring the requisite skills. She is in a variant of the learned helplessness trap described earlier. The key to unlocking the door to the needed new skills lies in altering her attitude. Often the key attitude is less manifest. In examples where the quiet rebel is having difficulties dealing with work colleagues, the attitudes which divert energies and hamper the acquisition of new interaction strategies may be hidden and inaccessible to change because unidentifiable. In these circumstances, do-it-yourself approaches are likely to fail.

SOCIAL SKILLS TRAINING

Communication with others requires social skills: knowledge of the rules which guide interaction and the ability to abide by them. As with motor skills—like riding a bicycle, building towers of cards, assembling electronic gadgets—some people are more skilled than others, and are more effective in attaining their desired goals. The social skills model of interaction assumes that there are optimum ways of behaving in social situations which represent a skilled performance. Social skills training is designed to teach people the optimum behaviours. It is, consequently, quite different from more generalised approaches which seek merely to alter the person's overall level of emotionality or habitual attitudes to problem solving. Social skills training is like a Mrs Beaton recipe: explicit in every detail, so that it is impossible to find a quiche lorraine in the oven that you thought contained an apple pie.

Deficits of social skill may mean that the person cannot cope well in particular social situations. This can mean being thrown into a vicious circle where failure to cope produces anxiety which further hampers skilled performances which accentuates anxiety and so on.

Social skills comprise verbal and non-verbal forms of communication and either can fail and produce stress. Non-verbal communication has been a particular focus of social skills training because it is a powerful channel for transmitting information that people tend to be less capable of monitoring for themselves. Non-verbal communication (NVC) includes bodily posture, gestures, facial expression, pattern of gaze, and so on. NVC is a vital ingredient of interaction: it is more salient than words in revealing information about the emotions; it is treated as more trustworthy than words, so that in clashes between what is said and what is expressed non-verbally, the latter wins normally; and it has an important role in pacing and sequencing talk. Looking is a particularly telling component of conversation. When two people look into each other's eyes (called 'eye contact') during a conversation, this acts as a cue for the person who has been talking to stop and the other to take over. The silent partner then carries on looking at the other, but the talker looks away until it is time to swap again or if there is need to check that the other is paying attention. Where the expected pattern of eye contact and looking does not occur, the conversation cannot flow; it has lost the lubricant which smoothes transitions. People who refuse to make eye contact or who stare continually disrupt normal interaction. They are considered to be shifty or frightening and elicit avoidance from others.

Normally, people learn the social skills expected in their culture of someone in their position during childhood social-isation. But sometimes this learning fails to take place, and then they do not know the rules or cannot apply them properly. Alternatively, people can move from one culture to another and the social skills learnt as a child become redundant. In some ways, the quiet rebel is like the cultural immigrant; she may not be equipped with the social skills necessary in her job, since she was not expected to do it and never educated for it before whatever formal training she had for it. Topping up on social skills might not be such a bad idea for the quiet rebel.

Social skills training has four stages: diagnosis of the nature of the skill deficit; re-education of specific behaviours, verbal and non-verbal; practice opportunities, using role play and psycho-drama; and, finally, performance in the real situation. The opportunity to practise the skill in role play where the costs of doing it wrong are minimal is important, not just to achieve a smooth performance but also to allow objective assessments of achievements by the trainer. Feedback on change is necessary in one form or another, which means that do-it-yourself social skills training is difficult. It is not impossible; even where role play in safety is not feasible, and skills have to be developed by trial and error on the job, the responses of co-workers can be used to monitor progress. Going-it-alone is probably not necessary, however, since there are innumerable short courses, in almost every locality, now run to develop social skills of all kinds: friendship skills; assertiveness skills; and so on.

One of the prime values of going on a short course is that you get the opportunity to role play not just yourself but other people, too. The woman manager could gain insight into the experience and feelings of a male subordinate by taking his role opposite someone acting hers. This process of 'taking the role of the other' can be like getting inside someone else's skin, because you start to see events from another perspective. Aspects of a situation which passed you by before, stand out with startling clarity. Your own behaviour is shaded by new hues and has different implications. You start to distinguish new paths of influencing events. People who are good communicators and effective managers of people tend to go through this ritual of taking the role of the other routinely. To them it is a standard step in deciding what they need to do. The quiet rebel could easily make this part of her routine, especially when dealing with difficult people. The acting out of the role of the other does not have to be literal; it can be done purely in the imagination by thinking through the situation from the other's viewpoint.

Standard social skills training can be aimed at any one or all of a number of targets. It can be designed to show that certain cues in a situation are vital, and how these should be interpreted. For instance, the cue concerned might be the proximity between the two people involved. Failure to understand that people normally require a basic minium of personal space that they can protect against intrusion may lead to breaches of those space requirements. Social skills training in that case would show when proximity stops being closeness and become intrusion. The interesting thing is that there are different cultural norms about proximity: low status people on the whole have smaller personal space requirements than those with high status; women require less than men on average; and so on. Where such cultural expectations clash, for instance in the case of the high status woman, the system breaks down and interaction is disrupted. The woman concerned, and through her anyone likely to break the proximity code, has to revise the interpretation of cues and learn new rules.

The second target for social skill training is the timing or sequencing of the interaction. Any reasonably ritualised pattern of interaction has a predictable sequence of components; misordering them is a heinous offence; like eating the dessert before the soup, it is indigestible. Mistiming or resequencing of components can be prevented once people are aware of the etiquette of that situation. For the quiet rebel, resequencing can be a deliberate strategy, self-consciously adopted to disrupt an interaction ritual which is problematic. In dealing with the 'Isn't she beautiful when angry?' ritual, she might start her offensive by saying that she knows she is attractive when angry and she is angry now. The pattern is shattered, and the man she is coping with has to use some other tactic.

The third target is the association between verbal and non-verbal elements of communication, which have to match to be maximally effective. When you are saying angry things, you have to look angry; anger has to emanate not just from your mouth but from your posture, gestures, and every atom of your presence. Any contradictions between the sources of information blurs the message and invites misinterpretation. Obviously, there are times when this is just what the socially skilled individual intends to achieve; it is a good technique for creating confusion and hiding real motives or opinions. The important thing is that skill implies control and organisation: for the skilled, such contradictions are deliberate tools of manipulation; when they occur unbidden, they signal lack of skill.

Most social skills training nowadays goes beyond instruction in fragments of behaviour (like when to break off eye contact, when to smile, or when to lean forward). The emphasis on discrete units of what has been called 'body language' has been superceded. Now training encompasses whole varieties of interaction, most notably work on *bargaining and negotiation*. Such training concentrates upon imparting to the trainee information about what the successful bargainer or negotiator does, and then requires emulation. The idea is that anyone can become more successful by following the formula. Again, teaching uses role play and practice with feedback before letting the person go solo in the real bargaining situation.

The bargaining formula might be interesting to the quiet rebel, whose position is often a matter of persistent re-negotiation even if her job does not require her to act in any formal capacity as a bargainer. Studies of poor bargainers have shown that they typically have a number of characteristics in common: they act with too little information in the mistaken belief that they understand the opponent's position; they make overreaching initial demands and ignore feedback from opponents; and they do not work out what would be an acceptable compromise position for themselves in advance. Successful negotiators, in contrast, make no assumptions about the opponent or the position the opponent will adopt. They do not assume anything about the opponent's knowledge base. They, consequently, explain everything about the situation as they understand it and they do this repeatedly, in several different ways, through any channels available. It is evident from this that they have no fear of building redundancies or repetition into their arguments, as long as they lay bare the underpinnings of the dispute. Having achieved that, and only then, do they move on to reconnoitring the bargaining range, feeling out what would or would definitely not be possible solutions. They seek at this stage to play down the degree of disagreement or extent of conflict of interests involved. Everything that can be done, is done to avoid antagonising the other unnecessarily. Placatory comments are followed by constructive suggestions about what concessions could be made, and the concessions offered are small and explicitly tied to similar concessions to be made in parallel by the opposition. Careful advance warning of which concessions might be forthcoming, through leaks or informal discussions or go-betweens, gives time for them to be considered by the opponent and they have a greater likelihood of success. Such negotiations are normally more successful, and a good track record, a history of making bargains that hold, makes subsequent efforts more likely to succeed.

There is no reason why the quiet rebel who needs to negotiate should not model herself on the successful bargainer, practising the components and refining her timing and sequencing in advance. Again, if she needs help, there are numerous short courses available.

The source for models of skilled social interaction does not have to be books or training courses. Traditionally people learned their social skills at work from watching other people do the job effectively, and most people still do it that way. The problem for the quiet rebel in using the traditional approach is that there may be no female model to emulate. She can try male models, but the social skills which work for them may not evoke the same responses when used by a woman. The congratulatory squeeze on the shoulder of a male subordinate by a man carries one set of social meanings, the same action by a woman means something else entirely—or can do, which is always the gamble. It therefore pays the quiet rebel to do a more formal and less intuitive or straight copycat analysis of the social skills required in her interactions at work.

Blocking Stress Management

All stress management methods are dependent upon the genuine efforts of the individual concerned. They rely upon honesty in the analysis of the source of stress, clarity in understanding one's emotional reaction, and persistence in learning new strategies and skills. Sometimes honesty, clarity and persistence are too much to hope for. People have different resources to call upon when coping with threats to the self. Some have poorer physical health initially. Some have very limited material resources; lacking money, time, or local facilities, for instance. Some have restricted social resources; they have less friends or relations who can rally around as support networks in times of stress. Some have low psychological resources; they have low self-esteem, few social skills, or no problem-solving skills. Any, and all, of these constraints on resources can mean that stress management is impossible in any serious way. The level of stress involved itself may be so great that coping strategies are disrupted. Honesty, clarity and persistence in the face of overwhelming problems may flee. The stress management methods are not magic potions bound to transmogrify the sufferer, and too often they are overpackaged and oversold by their proponents.

Stress management blocking can also be an unconscious but purposeful effort on the part of the sufferer. Succumbing to stress has its own allure. It means that you can give up the struggle but justifiably, because the odds are clearly overwhelmingly against you. Stress is the great get-out clause of our era. Failing in efforts at stress management can consequently be rewarding. Having tried at all just proves how valiant you are, but failure means you do not have to go on dealing with the stressful event, you can pull out bloodied and acceptably bowed. If the attractions of failure are greater than those of success, stress management will be blocked. Where stress management is failing for the quiet rebel, she might consider what advantages can be had from failure and whether they account for it.

Self-Esteem and Impression Management

Self-esteem is central to the dynamics of the self-concept; it is so important that people are very careful to encourage others to see them in a positive light. In reality, this entails impression management: projecting a particular image of one's self to others. The quiet rebel, whose self-esteem is likely to be continually under assault, has to become a past mistress of impression management. Impression management can rescue her from the prison of stereotypic roles and shield her against the backlash of mis-attributions.

Impression management can be regarded as a social skill: it requires a clear awareness of how others interpret actions and a wide range of self-presentation tactics. It also requires an ability to act in ways which need not be in accordance with the way you think of yourself. It may necessitate a whole series of lies and, if honesty is fundamental to your conception of yourself, there will be tension between your acts and your self-concept. Skilled impression managers can tolerate the strain. Yet it involves risks. It is possible to come to believe your own performance, particularly when everyone else believes it and treats you as if it were true. The distinction between the public and private realities gets lost somewhere along the way. The image is no longer managed, it is managing.

People who are good at managing impressions tend to monitor their own behaviour carefully and make careful observations of their impact on others. They consider themselves flexible and adaptive; they pay avid attention to information about others; and they like to take the dominant role in an interaction. They are adept at controlling the expression of their emotions through non-verbal cues and good at detecting any attempt by others at impression management. Such people like to know well in advance what type of situations they are likely to enter. They are very sensitive to the expectations of groups to which they belong, conforming in conforming groups, being radical in radical groups. It would be a fool who assumed that their actions indicated anything about their attitudes or beliefs.

This pattern has been labelled 'Machiavellianism' for obvious reasons. Studies have shown that 'High Machs' are usually very effective at influencing others and are not easily influenced themselves. They gain satisfaction from the sheer act of manipulating others and are willing to break almost any social expectation in the interests of self-gain. Children as young as ten years of age can be High Machs, and are normally the offspring of High Mach parents. It seems to be a manner of social interaction learnt very early and maintained effortlessly later; much to the consternation of Low Machs.

One of the prime functions of impression management, even when not taken to the lengths of the Machiavellian, is to gain social approval. In the search for approval, impression management utilises *ingratiation tactics* in the most outrageous ways. There are four major ingratiation tactics:

1. *Compliments*   Flattery is only effective if it can be made to appear spontaneous and credible. It is little use to have a lengthy and blatantly untrue statement prepared which you deliver off pat but which is irrelevant to the context in which it is delivered. Flattery works best with people who are insecure, but it must be discriminating: it is possible to devalue the currency of a compliment by using it with all and sundry.

Jackie, age fifty-four, newly promoted to a works director-ship of a light engineering factory, has learned the value of discriminating flattery. She says: 'Man management is

centrally about identifying what people value. I take time to get
to know what a man most loves before I offer him compliments
or try to use flattery to influence him. Once I know what he
values, I make sure that my compliments focus on that thing or
that person. If a man is proud of his daughter's academic
achievements, I make sure to ask about her and look impressed
with what he says. If you do this, you do not need to flatter him
broadly or insincerely.'

2. *Conformity*   Conformity with the opinions or behaviour of
the target for ingratiation can work as long as it appears
voluntary and is selective; undiscriminating agreement makes
your opinion worthless, but selective agreement gives the
appearance of judicial appraisal. Then it becomes important
only to disagree upon matters of no consequence while agreeing
consistently with all that are non-trivial.

Lesley, in her early twenties and in the publishing industry
as a production manager, echoes the ideas of many young
women striving for success: 'I learnt quickly that I am allowed
my own ideas and opinions in things that do not matter much.
In anything else I tow the line and, if anything, emphasise that
it was my view all along. I find most male managers never
notice if you fail to offer an opinion at first and then claim later
to have agreed with them all along, and even to have said so
earlier. There is a wilful gullibility about seeing others agree
with you.'

3. *Self-enhancement*   The objective here is to praise yourself
such that the target comes to recognise your great worth. Praise
has to be modulated to fit the target's own sense of self-worth:
the secure target is more responsive to efforts at self-glori-
fication; the insecure does not wish to be surrounded by anyone
better. Self-praise and self-deprecation require careful juxta-
position.

Gillian, in her mid-thirties, has learnt this lesson: 'I used to keep quiet about my successes at work. Virtue is its own reward, I thought. It wasn't. Now I am careful to make my virtues known. I do it subtly, I think, dropping it casually into conversations. I try to counterbalance it with some small expressions of self-criticism and self-doubt. I know it sounds terrible, but it is a game you have to play. You have to be your own public relations expert.'

4. *Rendering favours*   These have to be disguised so as to appear to have no ulterior motives, for this reason small, materially-insignificant favours can have the best effects. Gillian again points out that people are delightfully pleased with small unexpected gifts that cost her very little: 'I make sure to give away my excess apples and other fruit from the garden to people at work that I am softening up. Hard men crumble when faced with a cooking apple—so long as they have a wife or mother who will cook it.'

One could argue that ingratiation cannot be very effective, since people are aware of all of these tactics and will be alert against them. Strangely, very few people set out to examine how others try to ingratiate themselves, perhaps because they like to be ingratiated. There are powerful reasons not to notice that someone is trying to inveigle you into liking them; every ounce of vanity pushes that recognition under the carpet. In any case, ingratiation techniques work, and are there to be used when social approval is needed to bolster self-esteem during impression management.

In considering impression management, no evaluative stand should be taken. There is no point in saying that it is morally good or bad. Impression management is a skill, and it can be used for either good or ill; it is not often an end in itself. The quiet rebel will find that she has to deal with many people who are themselves highly skilled in the techniques of impression management. In order to deal with them effectively, it is useful to possess the same skills. In acquiring them the routine is the same as for any social skill: analyse the problem (in this case the target of influence); prepare your approach; practise; and perform for real. The roots of all good impression management are flexibility and sensitivity to feedback from others.

Self-esteem is important to healthy psychological functioning. Low self-esteem is related to loss of self-control, conformity to any and all situational demands, and the inability to function effectively in relationships. High self-esteem is tied to independence, consistency of behaviour across situations, and a feeling of integration and satisfaction. If impression management, no matter how distastefully manipulative, can procure self-esteem, its value has to be acknowledged.

There is one other thing to bear in mind: the search for high self-esteem does not sentence you to a lifetime of frantic impression management. High self-esteem, once established, tends to reduce the need for impression management. People with high self-esteem care less what others think about them. Such people select out information which supports their high regard for themselves. They learn rapidly and forget slowly things which gratify them; the rest is dross. Judicial, early use of impression management by the quiet rebel would be beneficial and should not be allowed to engender guilt.

Exercising the Self

At the heart of this chapter is the notion that the quiet rebel needs a strong self-concept. Self-maintenance, negativism, stress management and impression management are methods for creating such a healthy self-concept. The self-concept is like the body itself: if you exercise bits of it, they will become stronger. The quiet rebel needs the psychological muscle to fend off attacks launched by people who cannot accept that she should be different.

Self-exercises serve to develop greater control over the emotions and suggest specific problem-solving strategies. They are useful weapons for the quiet rebel to possess. The irony is that simply having them may mean that she does not have to use them. They may act as psychological deterrents. People, knowing that she can cope with stress, will not bother to test her; they may possibly even fear to do so.

Combined with the social and personal change strategies discussed in Chapter 8, self-exercises represent a formidable armoury. They do, however, require considerable effort. The consolation is that, just like any physical fitness programme, it gets less painful as you progress. Obviously, there is no cast-iron assurance that they all work for everyone. There is no promise that a 94-lb psychological weakling can be trans-formed into a Madam Universe. Yet gaining even a small portion of the analytical foresight and control of emotionality involved in all of the exercises will help. They all shift the balance of fate into your own hands.

Further Reading

Apter, M. J., *The Experience of Motivation: The Theory of Psychological Reversals*. London: Academic Press, 1982.

Lazarus, R. S. and Folkman, S., *Stress, Appraisal and Coping*. New York: Springer, 1984.

Argyle, M. (ed.), *Social Skills and Work*. London: Methuen, 1981.

Rubin, J. Z. and Brown, B. R., *The Social Psychology of Bargaining and Negotiation*. New York: Academic Press, 1975.

Jones, E. E., *Ingratiation*. New York: Appleton-Century-Crofts, 1964.

Goffman, E., *Relations in Public*. New York: Basic Books, 1971.

Priestley, P., McGuire, J., Flegg, D., Hemsley, V., and Welham, D., *Social Skills and Personal Problem Solving*. London: Tavistock Publications, 1978.

Chapter Eight
CHANGING OTHERS

The emphasis so far has really been upon how the quiet rebel might change herself, her behaviour, her feelings and her self-image, in order to succeed in her work. Yet, inevitably, there will be occasions when she will need to change others rather than herself. In her everyday dealings with other people, the quiet rebel is a force for change. Her very presence in her job breaches their expectations and challenges their preconceptions. Very often, if she is to survive and succeed, the quiet rebel will be called upon to change the attitudes of those around her. This chapter is designed to lay bare some of what psychologists have discovered about persuasion and the tactics for bringing about attitude change. Its purpose is to offer hints about how the quiet rebel might most effectively change the ways others treat her and think about her.

Becoming Persuasive

When it comes to persuading others, some people have a head start. We know, on the basis of a vast array of research, that the more powerful a person is, the more persuasive she is. Power can be derived from any of a series of attributes: possessing greater resources for reward or punishment of others; having sole possession of important information; being admired or respected; occupying a position which is invested with status. Power derived from any of these sources makes a person more persuasive. The problem for the quiet rebel is the difficulty she will probably have in gaining power in the first place. Without the ability to persuade others, she may not gain power; without power, she is less likely to be persuasive. A neat, self-perpetuating, and vicious circle you may think. However, there are other routes to persuasiveness. It is, for instance, worth noting that attractiveness has its own sort of power. People considered attractive by standards dominant in the culture concerned are found to be more persuasive. The attractive quiet rebel will have learnt long ago to capitalise upon this. Yet the quiet rebel who happens to have the double misfortune of lacking power and attraction need not despair. If she can establish a reputation for trustworthiness and credibility, this will act as a potent factor in making her persuasive. One's credibility can be maximised by being seen to go occasionally against one's own best interests in the pursuit of 'truth'. This sort of self-denial does not have to be frequent, but it can have a vast impact upon the way you are perceived.

Jessica, now a partner in a long-established law firm, describes her struggle for credibility and the importance of being persuasive: 'No one really doubted my knowledge of the law, or my specialism in commercial law, yet they doubted my ability to handle clients who were heads of large corporations. They felt I was more likely than a man to lose out in hard negotiations. They did not think I could be as effective in strenuous, long-run battles. I had to build up my credibility very slowly, proving myself able at each step. Any error on my part was a real setback, because errors counted far more than successes. I found I was having to use persuasion on three fronts: I had to persuade my firm that I should be trusted with important clients; I had to persuade the clients that I could handle the case; and I had to persuade any opponents that the client might have that my client was right. Over the years, I have learnt many persuasive tricks, but the first rule concerns credibility. Achieving credibility is a slow process but worthwhile.'

For most quiet rebels achieving credibility means sticking at the job and persisting, even when everyone and everything seems to be stacked against you. It is achieved through wearing down their resistance by repeatedly proving them wrong. Once some chink of credibility is established, you become more capable of persuading them that you are valuable and competent.

The effectiveness of persuasion is not simply determined by the power, attractiveness or credibility of the persuader. It also depends on what she says and does. As Jessica pointed out: 'You have to know when to use a one-sided argument to persuade someone and when to use a two-sided argument. One-sided arguments just put your own case and ignore the counter-argument; they work best with people who are slow on the uptake, or when they already really agree with you but just need a little bit more of a push. Two-sided arguments work better if the candidate for persuasion is smart and initially unconvinced that you are right. In this case, you put both sides of the argument, pro and con, but you make the cons sound weaker than they really are.' What Jessica has discovered from experience has received confirmation from psychological research. The two-sided argument seems to work on the inoculation principle: presenting views which oppose your own but in a watered-down fashion deprives them of their novelty and undermines their force. It is a strategy that all quiet rebels would find useful.

It's not what you say, it's the way that you say it

Persuasiveness is not just founded upon what you say, it also depends upon how you say it. Attempts at persuasion work best if you use them in face-to-face interactions: putting them in person, in the flesh, to the target for persuasion is most effective in bringing about change. For instance, a telephone conversation is less effective, and written communications least effective of all. The implication is clear: do not use the telephone or a letter in order to persuade someone if you can do it in person.

Features of the way you say a thing are not restricted to concern about the medium of its expression. The organisation of what you say is important in shaping its persuasive power. For instance, it has been found that people only basically remember the beginning and the end of lengthy arguments, they forget the middle. The implication is again clear: keep your attempts at persuasion short, or put the important things at the beginning and again at the end to maximise the amount people remember. This ties to another consistent finding that persuasiveness is massively improved by repetition and simple persistence. Saying something often, without any inconsistency, is persuasive. What you say does not have to be factually correct or even particularly logical, the sheer frequency of its use confers plausibility and generates acceptance. This may seem hard to believe. The only way to become personally convinced that it works is to try it and see. Zoe, who wants to be a film director and has, during her art studies, produced a number of short films, confirms its value: 'I've found that the way to sell myself as a film producer and director is to praise my own stuff. I sold something to an advertising agency by telling them over and over how wonderful it really was.'

Another persuasive tactic involves forewarning someone that you intend to try to persuade them. Surprisingly, warning someone in this way facilitates persuasion. It seems to work by disarming them, making them feel that you are not being underhand in your attempts to influence them. Jan, a printing trainee supervisor in a college specialising in crafts, claims: 'I am the only woman involved in the training of apprentices in the printing industry here. I work with some girl trainees and my major problem is persuading my fellow supervisors that these girls need the same training opportunities as the lads. They just seem to forget the girls when opportunities for interesting jobs arise. Anyway, I've developed a reputation as a champion of the girls. When persuading them to consider one of the girls for a job, I normally start by saying I intend to persuade them. They know then they are in for a telling . . . You know, it has another benefit, this business of warning them that I intend to persuade them. When I want to persuade them but don't warn them, they very rarely realise what I am up to, they have got so used to the frontal attack. Very often I succeed in changing their minds.'

Frightening them into Submission

Are people more likely to change their attitudes and behaviour if you frighten or threaten them? Many techniques of persuasion involve threats and take the form: 'If you do not do this, something terrible will happen to you'. Many advertising campaigns rely upon this formula: don't wear a seatbelt and your head will be smashed against the windscreen like a ripe peach; drink while pregnant and you will ruin the intellect of your child; smoke and you will destroy your attraction to the opposite sex; omit your deodorant and you will become a social outcast; and so on. The effects of threatening people in this way are not straightforward. Fear can both facilitate change, because people wish to avoid the prophesied punishment, and inhibit it, because people do not learn new things easily when they are anxious, or when they find the person attempting to persuade them unattractive and consequently less persuasive.

Persuasion which uses threats has to be carefully balanced: no fear means no motive to change, but too much fear generates a refusal to pay attention to what you are saying. What makes the calculation of optimal levels of threat so difficult is that people clearly differ in their responsiveness to fear in keeping with their habitual levels of anxiety. Some people are more anxious in a free-floating way all the time, and even a slightly frightening threat is likely to push them over the edge into a quivering unresponsive pulp.

The thing for the quiet rebel to do is to remember that fear arousal and threat can be used in the process of persuasion and that it should be a weapon in her arsenal, but it is one which needs to be tuned very carefully to the individual she needs to change. The most effective strategy is to adopt an experimental approach with new people, trying out different types of threat and different degrees of fear arousal. Such an approach clearly redounds with cynicism, but the quiet rebel wishing to succeed has to master all the arts of persuasion even if she later chooses to refrain from using some on ethical grounds.

Prime Targets for Persuasion

In any network of people, some individuals act as what are commonly called 'opinion leaders'. Typically, these are unusual in that they are open to new ideas and are willing to take risks in espousing them, acting as relaying channels to others who are less affected by initial attempts at propagating changed attitudes. Others rely upon the opinion leaders for information and prefabricated sets of beliefs; what they fail to pass on rarely actually reaches others. Consequently, the opinion leaders have to be the quiet rebel's prime targets for conversion and persuasion. They need to be identified, and a great effort should be directed at them in order to change their views about women in the job. Once they are persuaded, a ripple of changed attitudes should spread out from them to others in the workplace.

Tina is a twenty-eight-year-old civil engineer who works for a company which installs weaponry in military bases across the world; she consequently travels a great deal as part of a high-powered team of scientists and engineers. She discusses the importance of opinion leaders: 'I am the only woman in our team and, often, the only woman on the base where we find ourselves working. My team are used to me, but the construction workers and servicemen often find me anomalous. They do not know how to relate to me and try desperately to avoid dealing with me sometimes. Over the past three years, I have learnt that the best tactic is to identify who is acting as the informal leader of any gang and use my full persuasive powers to make him understand my role in the team first. It permeates down from him usually. Otherwise, I find myself seeking to convince too many people at once, and fighting the same tedious battles over and over again. Knocking out the king pin shortcuts the whole business.'

Attitudes and Actions

Many quiet rebels believe that they should be using persuasion to change the attitudes of those around them. They assume that if they could change attitudes towards themselves, they would of necessity be changing the way they are treated by others. This assumption is erroneous. There is no direct causal relationship between the attitudes a person holds and the behaviour she will exhibit. What a person ultimately does and says is the product of two sets of influences. On one side, there is the attitude towards the consequences of that act or talk which will be determined by the beliefs held about what the outcome will be and its value. On the other side, there is the way the person thinks other people will react to that action and the amount of importance allotted to their views. These two streams of influence precipitate how a person will intend to act in any given situation but, even then, intentions may not be carried out. Intentions can be subverted by circumstantial constraints. Consequently, there is many a slip between attitudes and action.

The quiet rebel who wishes to change attitudes towards herself has one main task, and that is to change beliefs about herself. She has to replace the set of beliefs which generate negative or inaccurate evaluations of herself with ones which are more accurate. She can achieve this by implementing the tactics of persuasion described earlier. However, if she also wishes to change how people act towards her, she has to do a second thing, and this is to try to change what the actor feels other important people think about his or her activities. For instance, she could show how people the actor admired or respected would consider the actions unfair or immoral, and so on. The objective is to show that mistreatment of her is not socially acceptable. Of course, this can be problematic when mistreatment of her can be virtually a social obligation, given the overall attitudinal climate.

Rebecca, a financier in her mid-fifties, describes the gulf she has experienced between attitudes and action: 'Often colleagues in other firms hold attitudes that are totally egalitarian. They believe that women who are qualified deserve equal opportunities. However, they fail to put this into practice. They will omit to offer a junior woman the training opportunities offered the young men, and she will often pass more slowly through the promotion process. Their explanations for their failure to carry out their good intentions are multitudinous: other firms don't do it, and they would disadvantage themselves when the woman had her "career break for children"; their directorate would not accept it; and so on. They are being constrained in their policy decisions by what they perceive to be socially expected or acceptable. In these cases, one is not fighting to change attitudes but to change how social constraints are perceived and accepted.'

There is one further point which deserves to be made regarding the relationship between attitudes and behaviour. The quiet rebel wishing to change both should remember that arguments designed to modify beliefs about herself should include specific recommendations for new ways in which she should be treated. The more specific the behavioural pre-scription, the more likely it is to be effective. Women wishing to gain equality of treatment should not just work in generalis-ations but be clear about the specific behaviours which should cease and what should supplant them. So, the quiet rebel should not call simply for equal opportunities, but should make it clear that she wants to be sent on a specific training course, or be able to attend specific conferences, or be provided with specific pieces of new equipment, or be consulted about a specific array of decisions, and so on. Specificity in the process of persuasion directs the way attitude changes are translated into modifications of action.

Unanticipated Side-Effects

The quiet rebel who seeks to change attitudes towards herself and the way she is treated will probably be motivated by purely personal concerns. She wants to be allowed to pursue her chosen career to the best of her ability. Any attitudinal or action changes she may induce will be brought about for her personal advantage. By definition, the quiet rebel is not interested in changing the position of all women; she is interested in her own position. Social change is not her objective; personal change is. Yet the pursuit of her personal development may have unanticipated side-effects. While her mere existence challenges social norms and stereotypes, her effect will be heavily accentuated once she sets about changing the attitudes of those around her. In effect, whether consciously or not, she will be introducing the seeds of social change.

There is no social movement which represents the interests of the quiet rebel. Quiet rebels are too heterogeneous to be easily sheltered by a single umbrella organisation. They are divided by age, class, education, race, religion, and geographical location. The characteristic that they have in common, a sexually atypical job, is not likely to be enough to bind them tightly to act in concert. In any case, the quiet rebel is not a joiner of groups, she is the archetypical individualist. Yet it is possible that the quiet rebel may undergo a metamorphosis. Some quiet rebels, having tried the personal route towards change and found it lacking, do become unquiet rebels. The transformation is rarely one of dramatic conversion. Gradually, over a period of years, the woman finds that her beliefs and attitudes change. She comes to recognise that any advances she personally can achieve are minimal, and that she should be fighting not just for herself but for other women as well. She recognises that unity is strength.

The problems and passions of the unquiet rebel are not the subject of this book. Suffice it to say that it would be foolish to regard the quiet rebel as someone who is static. The quiet rebel can become an unquiet rebel who will use all the tactics of social protest and propaganda normally associated with rebellion. She may not wish to, but she may be driven to it by the intransigence of problems to other methods. In fact, as long as her coping strategies work, the quiet rebel is likely to stay quiet.

Chapter Nine
THE QUIET REBEL

There are women now who are senior vice-presidents of vast
banking empires, marketing directors of multi-national corporations, and heads of influential law firms. There are women
who build helicopters and hovercrafts, design computers and
create weapons of biological warfare which can wreath the
Earth with megadeaths. There are women who have their
Master's ticket in the Merchant Marine, who drive railway
engines, and one who has captained a jumbo jet in scheduled
transatlantic service. There are women who have even
penetrated the élite craft industries of printing, motor
mechanics, and television camera work. All are examples of the
quiet rebel at work.

In each instance, the numbers of women who have arrived in
these jobs is small. None of them find that their lives are all a
bed of rose petals; more a bed of roses, thorns and all. Most
have been subjected to sexual discrimination at some time,
some suffer it most of the time. The women who aspire and
achieve in men's work seem to have a single attitude, at least, in
common. They feel that it is a tough world and it is hard for
anyone, male or female, to move ahead; nobody is doing
anybody any favours; if you perform, you make it, and if not,
you don't. This attitude reflects just how much they rely upon
their own resilience and talent. It resonates with the conviction

that effort is rewarded and merit is recognised, and that the individual can overcome prejudice whether personal or institutionalised.

It might be a little over-optimistic, but this attitude is necessary if the quiet rebel is to persist in her fight. If she believes that individual struggle is set at nought, she is unlikely to bother at all. A deep-seated individualism is a strong foundation for the quiet rebel's actions. Perhaps it is that which enables her to break with tradition and break into her chosen occupation. It is almost certainly that which makes her rebellion quiet, a personal affair, not tied to any vehement support for mass social movements or adherence to political doctrine. She does the job which she has chosen not as a gesture or protest against patriarchy intended to change the position of all women. She does it because she personally wishes to do it. That this may mean shifting the status of all women is incidental. She is the cornerstone of social change, but not intentionally. She is radical most often only in her individualism, and this may be restricted solely to her working life. Radicalism is not a quality she would claim. She may well be sick and tired of others trying to tar her with the brush of radicalism with all its pejorative feathery connotations.

Isolation is the natural bedfellow of individualism. The quiet rebel, regardless of the nature of her work, reports isolation, feeling the absence of female peers particularly acutely. Organisation can overcome isolation. For instance, in 1978 a small group of professional women working in the City of London, who wanted to find a way in which women in 'senior positions, often lacking peers in their own companies' could share common interests and solve mutual problems, created the City Women's Network. The network represents a variety of professions and industries, but mostly traditional city institutions like law and banking. One of its aims is to encourage women to seek executive, managerial and professional positions, but it is not a group of militants pressuring government for political changes in legislation on equal opportunities or anything of that sort. It functions as an informal network of contacts: something like a nascent young girls' network to parallel that of the old boys. This sort of grassroots development of an organisation for women with similar occupational aspirations may be more effective in the long-run than those superimposed by government departments through training schemes and short courses. Such organisations impose no ideological framework and make only limited personal demands, and they are ideal for the ardent individualist who happens to dislike isolation. Support without interference, advice without dogma; who could ask for more? The unquiet rebel might, of course. The unquiet rebel would see her own future as attainable only as part of a mass movement in the status of all women. Fortunately for the *status quo*, there do not seem to be all that many unquiet rebels around.

Crises for the Quiet Rebel

Most quiet rebels will confront common crisis points: times when decisions of great importance have to be made. They are the same sorts of decisions that everyone else makes, they just become more problematic for the quiet rebel because her choice is not pre-recorded by tradition or custom. It is at these crisis points that she becomes acutely aware that she is different and rebellious, no matter how quiet. The rest of the time the unusualness of her position and aspirations can be played down. When life decisions have to be made, they zoom into focus. These crisis points will normally include the initial job choice; questions of whether to marry, and if so when; whether to have children and, if she does, how many; whether to have a long period of absence away from work in mid-career for child-rearing; whether to remain geographically mobile in the interests of career development despite family commitments; how to deal with outright discrimination in access to or promotion in a job; and which of the spectrum of typecast roles on offer at work to choose, if any.

Crises can be sources of strength as well as of defeat. Success in dealing with a crisis is a tremendous psychological tonic. Each one which is met and passed successfully enhances the likelihood of subsequent success. Ironically, the more crises people have to deal with, within limits, the better they are at coping with stress and with their own and others' emotional reactions to it. The skills, of course, have to be acquired in the first place, and part of the purpose of this book has been to describe skills and offer information which might be useful in practising them.

It is unfortunate for the novice at coping with crises involving hard decisions which need complex negotiation with and persuasion of others, that many of them congregate at the start of her career. The young quiet rebel has all the decisions about home and work roles to make within an abbreviated period of time, and it is rarely possible to prevaricate to her own advantage. Some of the crises may be recurrent (every time you change jobs a new work persona has to be renegotiated), but never again will they pile so high all at once. It is clear that at this time the quiet rebel is most in need of help. It is then that she needs to acquire the skills to cope. It is tempting to say that all training courses designed to deliver women into men's work should include a hefty section on such skills. Women are becoming a valuable economic commodity, as they comprise more and more of the labour force, and courses which train them to *do* the job but not to *survive* in the job are an expensive waste of time.

This plea for the training of coping skills should not be taken to imply that there is any firm evidence that women are more likely than their male counterparts to fail in their chosen career. However, those surveys which have been done show that the social cost women pay for success in men's work is higher. They are breaking new ground and sometimes it retaliates, crushing them or opening like a chasm at their feet.

Training individuals to cope better is only one side of the equation; the other must include changes in social attitudes, legislation and institutional structures which will enable them to function effectively and implement coping strategies realistically. Simple, if costly, legislative and organisational changes could make crises evaporate. Flexi-time to allow dual career couples to share child-care; crèches in industrial sites for women who wish to return to work soon after childbrith; variations in the maternity/paternity leave allowances; positive discrimination in training, and single-sexed training courses; and so on, all would smooth the path of the quiet rebel.

Perhaps too much emphasis has been placed on the younger quiet rebel and her decision crises. The problems of the established and middle-aged quiet rebel are rarely mentioned. The older woman has crises which are just as important: she has to manage teenagers, promotion responsibilities, her own menopause, not to mention her spouse's male menopause; and, increasingly, divorce. Things do not get all that much easier for the quiet rebel as she gets older; she just has the experience to handle them better. Nevertheless, some of the skills of persuasion and attitude change, impression management, and stress management described earlier might be valuable. They are not universal panaceas, just scraps of help—rags to polish skills you may already possess without ever having thought of them in any formal or systematic way. The art of psychology is to make people truly aware of what they then realise they know already.

Halos and Horns

It is often believed that the great innovators, the trail-blazers, the women who first break into a male domain, have the most horrendous difficulties with which to deal. The wondrous stories of the first female doctors and scientists confirm this sort of image. At the time, the problems are doubtless momentous enough, but in retrospect a strange metamorphosis occurs. Being one of the very first has a glamour that is its own reward. Total uniqueness can be sustaining, and such women often arise saint-like in their fortitude and courage amidst their woes. They acquire a personal mythology; their exploits and attitudes are recounted with awe and send shivers of trepidation down the spines of women who would tread in their footsteps. Their halos shine forth, especially once they are retired or, better still, dead. The men who once worked with them describe them in hallowed tones. Women who follow after are led to understand that they could never be expected to attain such dizzy heights of perfection. Perfection recognised, of course, in retrospect, so that the woman concerned is hardly benefited except in memory. By her standard other women are failures before they even begin. This is, obviously, where the sting in the tail of all this posthumous reverence is revealed. Canonisation of the early women in a field makes their achievements an unrealistic target for subsequent women. It acts simultaneously as discouragement and degradation for newcomers, minimising their efforts and abilities, emphasising their deficiencies. The halos of the old guard illuminate the horns of their successors.

The quiet rebel has to resist the folklore and fable of her workplace; she should absorb it, read it for its underlying meanings and messages, but she should not believe it. She cannot afford to allow her self-concept to be adorned with horns. She is no devil, just as her predecessors were no saints. She is just a woman doing a job.

Index